THE SOUTHERN WAY

C000224527

CONTENTS

Editorial Introduction	5
Southern Railway Portsmouth Line Corridor Stock Part 2	6
The Story of EMU Names	31
Rail-Tour Heaven	32
The Ashford 1948 Wagon Photographs	40
New Locomotive Depot at Ashford	52
The last of the Ashford 'C's.	57
Take 2 (and a bit)	61
A Survey of Southampton's Railways. Part 1 : Woolston to Redbridge	62
'Rebuilt' - The Letters and Comments pages	79
Ave Atque Vale .... Hayling Farewell	87
Alice Tubbs of Durley	96
A little local difficulty...	99
Somerset & Dorset Joint: Part 1 Radstock to Shepton Mallet	100
Defeated by the Drains	106
Book Review 'Southern Style: Part One London & South Western Railway'	110
Southern Railway Traffic Officers Conference: 28 March 1938	111
Terry Cole's Rolling Stock File No 30	116
The Funeral Train of Sir Winston Churchill	118
Did steam really end at midnight on Sunday 9 July 1967?	120

© Kevin Robertson (Noodle Books) and the various contributors 2015
ISBN 978-1-909328-33-4
First published in 2015 by Kevin Robertson
under the **NOODLE BOOKS** imprint
PO Box 279
Corhampton
SOUTHAMPTON
SO32 3ZX
www.noodlebooks.co.uk
editorial@thesouthernway.co.uk

Printed in England by Berforts Information Press Ltd.

Leaning to the curve at Waterloo, 1-Co Co-1 No 10202 awaits departure with a Bournemouth line service in the early 1950s. (For more information on the use of the three SR main-line diesel-electric locos, see 'S/Way Special issue No 1' which is devoted to the type and also an article within 'S/Way Special issue No 10.'.

Amyas Crump

Editorial

This is the second attempt at an Editorial piece for this issue. Usually this page is one of the first items to be compiled, I suspect as much a psychological move on my part whereby once the first bit of writing is complete then the rest just seems to fit and follow. Plan? - there is one (of sorts), I know what there is available and somehow it all seems to fit in to form a cohesive edition, well I hope so anyway. This time though instead of being the first item ready it is actually the very last. I will admit on this occasion I had been a bit stuck on what to say, that is until late in the day for the inclusion of material for this issue the necessary components for 'The Funeral Train of Sir Winston Churchill' arrived and when put together revealed a question I am unable to answer.

There was also insufficient space on pages 118-9 to raise this so here would seem an appropriate place.

The information we have shows that the van selected to act as a hearse was inspected in July 1962, two-and-a-half years ahead of when it would actually be needed. However, before anyone gains the impression this was rather macabre advance preparation, do remember that in June 1962 when already aged 88, Sir Winston Churchill had fallen out of bed and broken his hip whilst staying at a hotel in Monte Carlo. There was fear for his life and having publically stated that he wished to die in England, he was rapidly transported back home courtesy of the RAF. In fear of his long term survival it was for this reason that plans were rapidly put into place to deal with his eventual demise, one small but significant part of which was the selection of a suitable rail vehicle that would carry the coffin.

PMV No. S2464 had been in store at Worthy Down sometime since November 1961 and was reported as officially withdrawn. Having been inspected on 3 July 1962 and selected as suitable, the railway moved fast, for soon afterwards at Stewarts Lane (a further paint date showed 'July 1965') it had been made ready and was repainted in Pullman colours - stored with instructions "Not to be used under any circumstances whatsoever until authorised". (It was subsequently repainted, again in Pullman style on 20 January 1965.)

Turn again now to pages 118-119 and we learn two interesting facts, firstly that on 3 July van No. S2464 was stored in position at Worthy Down close to the severed connection of this wartime spur near to Winchester Junction, also that the same spur line had been severed at the Worthy Down end. All the vehicles here were thus in effect isolated. They were also suffering from the effects of vandalism.

To extract the selected vehicle would have been impractical from the main line end at Winchester Junction - not least as there was certainly nowhere for an engine to run round at this point, whilst in addition it would certainly have been needed to be inspected as fit to travel. The option then was to reinstate the connection at Worthy Down and carrying out a rather lengthy and involved shunt. Certainly easier here, as by this time the DNS route was freight only, passenger services having been withdrawn in March 1960.

What we do not know is how soon after 3 July this took place but clearly it was fast. I am fortunate in having on the shelf a full set of the weekly Special Traffic Notices for the area and period in question and yet there is nothing mentioned. There would certainly have been a need to despatch an engine from Eastleigh whilst it would probably also have taken several hours to secure the release of the van.

With nothing mentioned about a special working or indeed a similar special movement as ECS from Eastleigh to Clapham Junction/Stewarts Lane, the conclusion must be that this was made under what the Western used to describe as 'box to box' communication, i.e. following a telephone notification from control or a printed daily sheet of additional special workings. I would certainly love to know more (not least as many will know I do have certain affinity for the DNS!)

The point I would make over all this is simple, Railways are not just about parliamentary dates, openings, timetables, locomotive dimensions, rolling stock numbers and timetables, most, if not all, of these facts are well recorded in history. What though has slipped through the net is detail of the special and unusual workings, especially the day to day changes and extra trains. Rarely perhaps did they have such important historic significance as in the extraction of van No S2464, but each of these odd pieces of paper could add so much to our knowledge of railway history. Please, if you have acquired copies of Special Traffic Notices especially these 'short notice' workings, do make sure their future is assured and if you own a great wad how about a bit of digging to see if it is possible to put together what is a jigsaw of information into a cohesive story.

Personally I spend one evening with a copy of Terry Bye/Glen Woods' reports on my knee and the bound copies of the Weekly Special Traffic Notice to hand in order to come up with the above. (There was still space for a cup of tea on the table as well so you do not take over the whole house.) Was it worth it? I think so. I hope others will agree likewise.

Kevin Robertson

Front cover - *Another of David Williams' superb colour renditions. 'C3' No 2304 seen at Norwood junction shed. Built in 1906 this was the first member of the class to be withdrawn in 1936.*
Pages 2/3 - *Brand new D65xx (later Class 33) approaching Stoke Junction with tank wagons from Grain in December 1961. Roger Holmes*
Rear cover - *Motor Brake Second of former 4COR unit No 3087 but seen here when performing duty as departmental unit No 054 - see entry on p26.*

Above - COR sets in opposite platforms at Waterloo and displaying new and old liveries. From the presence of the red blind, set No 3136 has clearly recently arrived at its destination. Recall also the then practice of passengers in a rush alighting and not closing the door behind them.
R F Roberts

Left - Interior of a third-class restaurant car in a Portsmouth four-car set. Years later we wonder slightly at the ability of the staff (and passengers') to order, serve and consume what could well be a three course meal in the limited time it took to travel between Waterloo and Portsmouth.

SOUTHERN RAILWAY
PORTSMOUTH LINE CORRIDOR STOCK

4RES / 4BUF / 4COR / 4GRI / 4PUL / 4COR(N) Corridor Units (Part 2)

John Atkinson with contributions from Colin Watts

(Continued from S/Way No 29)

4 BUF Units 3072 - 3085

Numbered 3073 - 3085, the thirteen 4-BUF units were delivered in 1938 between May and July when they were introduced into service. These units comprised two motor brake thirds (identical to those in the 4-RES and 4-COR units) a buffet car (seating unclassified) and a trailer composite.

Each 4-BUF unit was 264' 6" long and weighed 162¾ tons and had a total seating capacity of 30 first and 128 third plus 26 unclassified seats in the buffet car. The units were constructed at Eastleigh works and released to traffic from May 1938, units 3073 - 3079 dated May 1938 and 3080 - 3085 dated June 1938.

The Buffet Cars

The buffet car consisted of a vestibule with outward opening doors each side, kitchen area, bar area with ten column-mounted stools arranged along a counter, a dining saloon with sixteen chairs (arranged as four chairs around four specially shaped tables), a partition with double swing doors leading to a further vestibule again with entrance doors each side and two lavatories (one either side of a central corridor). The coach had no windows in the bar area, only a small sliding ventilator behind the counter area, and weighed 37 tons 2cwt. It was to diagram No. 2601.

The buffet car was marshalled with the kitchen end against the motor coach and the corridor past the kitchen was to the nearside when that motor coach was leading in direction of travel. A swing door was located in the corridor past the kitchen area. Ten stools along the bar were located against an arc in the bar counter so each customer had their own arc. The tables were similarly shaped with four arcs in each with the chairs suitably located, each table being located against a large sidelight window and provided with a table lamp.

There were four large sidelight windows along the corridor side of the coach, unevenly spaced with two along the corridor past the kitchen, the other two by the tables in the dining saloon. Only one of these originally had a two piece sliding vent above, this being the one nearest the kitchen area. Later, the two at the saloon end were modified with BR style sliding ventilators. Partitions and decorative wall mouldings in the coach replicated the 'arc' theme of the tables and bar counter. Power for the kitchen equipment was provided by a motor generator set mounted below the underframe.

The buffet cars were staffed by crews from the Pullman Car Company Limited with stores loaded at Bognor and Victoria. Due to wartime restrictions, the buffet cars were removed from all units for the period from 22nd May 1942 until 7th January 1946 when all refreshment facilities were suspended, and the units operated as three-car sets. The buffet cars were stored on the Crystal Palace (High Level) branch for some time.

Trailer Composite

The trailer composite was to the same internal layout as those in the 6-PUL units with a side corridor joining five 7' 1¾" wide first and three 6' 3" wide third class compartments with a lavatory at each end; seating 30 first and 24 third class passengers. It weighed 32½ tons and was to diagram No. 2309.

Each compartment had its own access door on the non-corridor side, whilst there were five doors along the corridor side. These were located unevenly along the coach; one opposite the partition of the first and second first-class compartments, one opposite the doorway of the centremost compartment and one opposite the partition of the fourth / fifth first-class compartments (three in total) as well as two more doors opposite each of the partitions of the third-class compartments. A swing door in the corridor separated the first and third class sections of the coach. Smoking in first-class was allowed in the first compartment at the end of the coach and the two at the other end of the group of five compartments, whilst only the centremost of the three third-class compartments was non-smoking.

4 BUF Unit 3072

After conversion from a 4-RES unit in 1956, unit 3072 now reclassified as a 4-BUF remained non-standard with the other units as the cafeteria car seated 36 in unclassified seats and the former dining first now seated 42 first-class as the original dining area was now regarded as ordinary first class seating. The unit therefore seated 42 first, 104 second and 36 buffet. The buffet car weighed 35 tons, so 3072 weighed 160¾ tons overall. It remained working on the Waterloo - Portsmouth route.

4 BUF Liveries

When delivered the buffet cars were painted in the lighter 'Malachite' green livery, the remaining three coaches being the normal darker olive green colour and a large 'Southern' legend at sliding vent height, with 'Buffet Car' below at waist height painted on the windowless area of the coach. However, the buffet cars were later painted olive green to match the remainder of the unit. Dates for these repaints are sought!

Units were painted green when new, repaints from January 1964 having a small yellow warning panel added on the corridor end, but from January 1967 were repainted into all-over blue with full yellow ends, unit 3078 receiving the intermediate livery of blue ends with small yellow panel, though it was painted blue again and became standard in May 1969. Unit 3076 was the last in green livery, being painted blue in August 1969.

4 BUF Demise and Withdrawal

The units remained in service on the Mid-Sussex line route to Portsmouth and saw lesser use on the main Brighton line, units receiving their routine maintenance at Streatham Hill, but from 4th January 1964 nine units (3073-78/80-82) were displaced by 4-BEP units and transferred to the Waterloo - Portsmouth route displacing the twelve

surviving 4-RES units, though working alongside the three 4-GRI units and non-standard cafeteria car unit 3072. They remained in service on this line until withdrawal and replacement by new 4-BIG units in 1970-1, now being based at Fratton depot for maintenance although some work was also undertaken at Wimbledon Park.

However, three units (3083-85) remained on the Central Division for use in business trains. Eight units were withdrawn in November 1970 upon introduction of new 4 BIG units though 3082/3 were out of use by 10th October 1970, and 3072 and the three 4-GRI units then moved to the Central division. The four surviving Central units (3075/7/80/5) moved to the South Western where they remained in traffic as non-buffet units on the Reading line until the end of January 1971 when all were stored at Wimbledon Park until withdrawal in March 1971. The last catering services using 'Portsmouth' stock ceased on 30th April 1971 and 3072 was then stored at Gatwick along with 4-GRI units 3086-8. These four were withdrawn officially from 20th November 1971. Withdrawn units were stripped of equipment at Selhurst Repair Shop prior to disposal.

Unit no. Diag no.	MBT 2114	TRB 2602	TCK 2505	MBT 2114	Withdrawn	Notes
Code	A	BC-1A	BD	A-1A		Codes allocated from c.1963
3072	11175	12613	12244 *	11176	20-Nov-71	Ex 4 RES in 1956 * TFK
Code	A-1A	BE	BA	A		Codes allocated from c.1963
3073	11120 11121	12518 12519	11846	11229 11148 11122	21-Nov-70	
Code	A	BE	BA	A-1A		Codes allocated from c.1963
3074	11232 11213 11172	12519 10071² 12518	11847	11231	21-Nov-70	² Diagram 2009, Code BB (4 COR TSK).
3075	11234	12520	11848	11233	13-Mar-71	
3076	11236	12521	11849	11235	21-Nov-70	
3077	11238	12522	11850	11237	13-Mar-71	
3078	11240	12523	11851 11856	11239 11249 11145	21-Nov-70	
3079	11242	12524	11852	11241	30-Nov-63	
3080	11244 11250	12525	11853	11243	13-Mar-71	
3081	11246 11177	12526	11854	11245	21-Nov-70	
3082	11248	12527	11855	11247 11206	21-Nov-70	
Unit no. Diag no.	MBT 2114	TRB 2601	TCK 2309	MBT 2114	Withdrawn	Notes
Code	A	BE	BA	A-1A		Codes allocated from c.1963
3083	11250 11112 11205	12528	11856 11851	11249 11191	21-Nov-70	
3084	11252	12529	11857	11251	21-Nov-70	
3085	11254	12530	11858	11253	13-Mar-71	

	Individual Unit Notes 3072 - 3085
3072	Unit non-standard in formation, weight and seating capacity as included TFK instead of TCK and seated 42 first, 104 second and 36 buffet. TRS 12613 now converted to a 36 seat cafeteria car with the former kitchen end unchanged and the dining saloon altered to a 5½ bay area with loose chairs at tables arranged two-aside each side of the central gangway with the odd ½ bay at the inner end of the saloon. The Diagram No. of the TRB was amended to 2602 and the unit then weighed 160¾ tons.
	Unit ran temporarily in late 1956 with Pullman car Brenda (ex 3013) for bogie trials in connection with the bogie replacement programme for the 6-PUL and 5-BEL units, the unit making a test run from Lancing to Redhill on 2ⁿᵈ November 1956 in this formation.
	Despite the non-standard features, this unit outlasted the other 4-BUF units and was withdrawn along with the three 4-GRI units 20-Nov-71 as the last remaining catering 'Portsmouth' stock, though the last use of all four of these units was in May-71.
	Unit then stored briefly at Ford then moved to Gatwick from 8-May-71 for almost a year until 5-May-72 when taken to Selhurst for stripping and three coaches sold for scrapping at T. W. Ward, Beighton, moving from Norwood Yard 24-Jun-72.
	TRB 12613 sold for use as a transport cafe in goods yard at Wood Lane, Shepherds Bush from 17-Jun-72, moving from Norwood Yard to Sterne Street 27-Sep-72, believed scrapped in 1974 following fire damage. [*See also 4 RES section*].
3073	Unit damaged by enemy incendiaries at Streatham Hill 28-Sep-40 and three coaches badly burnt. TRB 12518 withdrawn 11-Dec-40 and body scrapped with underframe being used as basis for ship's gangway carrying vehicle at Southampton Docks from May-54. This vehicle later allocated 'Internal User' number IU080336. (*possible this vehicle still exists at the Swanage Railway?*).
	MBT 11229 and TCK 11846 damaged but repaired and 11229 to 3070 and replaced by 11148 (ex 3058) from 1-Sep-41. Unit ran as 3-COR until insertion of TRB 12519 (ex 3074) from Dec-46, when unit reverted to 4 BUF.
	Unit defective and TRB 12519 used briefly in 3144 during May-57.
	Unit withdrawn 21-Nov-70 and both MBSs 11148 and 11230 to 3121. Replaced by MBSs 11121 and 11122 (ex 3121) and unit sent for storage at Micheldever, arriving 12-Feb-71 with both MBSs moved for scrapping 11-May-71 to T. J. Thomson, Stockton from there. TRB 12519 and TCK 11846 both to Hoo Jct c.16-Mar-71 from Oatlands Siding where their bodies were broken-up and the underframes sent to Stewarts Lane c.Dec-71; the underframe of 11846 then being used for basis of long-welded-rail carrying wagon DB975521. Underframe of 12519 not so used and cut-up at Tonbridge West Yard by 20-Jan-73.
3074	Unit damaged by enemy action (*date & location unknown*) and after repairs MBT 11232 to 'new' unit 3156 from Jul-46. TRB 12519 to 3073 from Dec-46. 11232 replaced by 11213 (ex 3148) and unit ran as 3 COR until made up to 4-COR May-46 with new TTK 10071, this vehicle built to replace war losses and transferred to 'new' 3117 Nov-46.
	A new 12518 built Oct-48 when unit reverted to 4-BUF.
	Unit in collision with 6-PUL 3009 at Lovers Walk 10-Sep-64 and 11213 wrecked and withdrawn 27-Aug-66, (*probably broken-up at Lovers Walk*). Replaced by 11172 (ex Push-Pull tests; formerly in 3059).
	Unit withdrawn 21-Nov-70 and initially stored at Barnham prior to stripping at Selhurst before moving to Micheldever (arriving 10-Feb-71) for storage; both MBSs 11172 and 11231 moved for scrapping 11-May-71 to T. J. Thomson, Stockton from there.
	TRB 12518 and TCK 11847 both to Hoo Jct c.16-Mar-71 (from Oatlands Siding) where their bodies were broken-up and the underframes sent to Stewarts Lane c.Dec-71; the underframe of 11847 then being used for basis of long-welded-rail carrying wagon DB975520. Underframe of 12518 not so used and stored in Battersea Yard from Dec-71, moving to Tonbridge West Yard for cutting up by 3-Jan-72.
3075	Unit new to traffic 23-May-38. Unit withdrawn 13-Mar-71 and initially stored in Wimbledon South Sidings before moving to Selhurst for stripping 30-Jun-71. After stripping unit stored at Micheldever and moved for scrapping from there 27-Sep-71 to A King Ltd, Wymondham.
3076	Unit withdrawn 21-Nov-70 and after stripping at Selhurst sent for storage at Micheldever arriving 12-Feb-71, both MBSs moved for scrapping 11-May-71 to T. J. Thompson, Stockton from there.
	TRB 12521 and TCK 11849 both to Hoo Jct c.16-Mar-71 (from Oatlands siding) where their bodies were broken-up and the underframes sent to Stewarts Lane c.Dec-71; the underframe of 11849 then being used for basis of long-welded-rail carrying wagon DB975522. Underframe of 12521 not so used and stored in Battersea Yard from c.Jan-72 moving to Tonbridge West Yard for cutting up by 19-May-73.
3077	Unit withdrawn 13-Mar-71 and initially stored in Wimbledon South Sidings before moving to Selhurst for stripping 7-May-71, thence hauled to Gatwick 10-Jul-71 for storage. Unit moved to Channelsea Jct Sep-71 and from there to Whitemoor Yard 1-Oct-71 and forward for scrapping to A King Ltd, Wymondham arriving Dec-71.

3078	Unit damaged by enemy bombing at Bognor 11-Apr-41 and MBT 11239 and TCK 11851 badly affected. After repairs MBT 11239 to 3150 from Apr-45, TCK 11851 to 3083 from Aug-43. Replaced from May-41 by 11249 and 11856 (both ex 3083). At some stage, unit had the ten stools along the bar area in TRB 12523 removed, reducing the seating capacity by ten to sixteen, overall unit capacity now being 30 first, 128 second and 16 buffet. Unit 'ran-away' in Selhurst Depot 17-Aug-70 and MBS 11240 damaged in collision with depot wall. Unit withdrawn 21-Nov-70 and MBS 11249 to 3163 and exchanged with defective 11145 and after stripping at Selhurst unit to Micheldever for storage arriving 21-Sep-70. Both MBSs to Eastleigh 11-Dec-70 but returned to Micheldever 18-Feb-71. Both MBSs 11145 and 11240 moved for scrapping 11-May-71 to T. J. Thomson, Stockton from there. TRB 12523 and TCK 11856 both to Hoo Jct c.16-Mar-71 (from Oatlands siding) where their bodies were broken-up and the underframes sent to Stewarts Lane c.Dec-71; the underframe of 11856 then being used for basis of long-welded-rail carrying wagon DB975523. Underframe of 12523 not so used and stored in Battersea Yard from c.Dec-71 moving to Tonbridge West Yard for cutting up by 14-Oct-72.
3079	Unit in collision with 6-PAN 3023 in New Cross Gate sidings 27-Sep-62 and MBS 11242 and TRB 12524 badly damaged; unit to Micheldever for storage by Dec-62. Both vehicles were subsequently withdrawn, 11242 scrapped at Eastleigh Jun-63, 12524 to Eastleigh for repairs but deemed beyond economic repair and probably scrapped there Dec-64 (*coach deleted from records 2 W/E 19-Dec-64*). Unit deleted from 30-Nov-63. MBS 11241 and TCK 11852 repaired by Oct-63 and stored at Micheldever until both to 3134 from Apr-64.
3080	Unit damaged by enemy action during 1942 (*date & location unknown*) and after repairs MBT 11244 to 3101 from Dec-44. Replaced by 11250 (ex 3083). MBS 11243 collision damaged (*where?*) Sep-62 but repaired. Unit withdrawn 13-Mar-71 and initially stored in Wimbledon South Sidings before moving to Selhurst for stripping 7-May-71 thence hauled to Gatwick 10-Jul-71 for storage. Unit moved to Channelsea Jct Sep-71 thence to Whitemoor Yard 1-Oct-71 and forward for scrapping to A King Ltd, Wymondham arriving Dec-71.
3081	Unit damaged by enemy bombing at Bognor 11-Apr-41 but repaired. MBS 11246 damaged in collision with 3161 at Wimbledon Park late 1968 and exchanged with 11177 (ex 3161). Unit withdrawn 21-Nov-70 and initially stored at Barnham prior to stripping at Selhurst, thence moving to Micheldever arriving 10-Feb-71 for storage with both MBSs 11177 and 11245 moved for scrapping 11-May-71 to T. J. Thompson, Stockton from there. TRB 12526 and TCK 11854 both to Hoo Jct c.16-Mar-71 (from Oatlands Siding) where their bodies were broken-up and the underframes sent to Stewarts Lane c.Dec-71; the underframe of 11854 then being used for basis of long-welded-rail carrying wagon DB975525. Underframe of 12526 not so used and stored in Battersea Yard from c.Dec-71 moving to Tonbridge West Yard for cutting up by 19-May-73.
3082	Unit damaged by enemy bombing at Bognor 11-Apr-41 and MBT 11247 badly affected, after repairs to 'new' unit 3158 from Jan-46. Replaced c.May-41 by 11206 (ex 3144). Unit out of use from 10-Oct-70 and stored at Ford from 17-Oct-70. Unit withdrawn 21-Nov-70 and moved to Gatwick 8-May-71 for further storage. Unit to Selhurst for stripping 2-Dec-71 and moved for scrapping Jan-72 from Norwood Yard to A King Ltd, Wymondham.
3083	Unit damaged by enemy bombing at Bognor 11-Apr-41 and MBT 11250 and TRB 12528 badly affected but repaired. MBT 11249 and TCK 11856 both to 3078 from May-41. MBT 11250 to 3080 after repairs. Replaced by MBT 11112 (ex 3116), TCK 11851 (ex 3078), MBT 11191 (ex 3137) from Aug-43. Unit out of use from 10-Oct-70 and stored at Ford from 17-Oct-70. Unit withdrawn 21-Nov-70 and moved to Gatwick 8-May-71 thence on to Wimbledon Park 15-May-71 for stripping. MBS 11112 to 3144 from 12-Jun-71 and exchanged with damaged 11205. Unit then moved to Micheldever 15-Jul-71 before moving (21-Sep-71) for scrapping to A King Ltd, Wymondham.
3084	Unit withdrawn 21-Nov-70 and moved to Gatwick 8-May-71 for further storage. Unit to Selhurst for stripping 2-Dec-71 where TRB 12529 removed, remaining three coaches moved for scrapping Jan-72 from Norwood Yard to A King Ltd, Wymondham. TRB 12529 claimed as part of the National Collection (officially from 3-Jun-72) and later (after a period in store at Preston Park) moved to York 3-Dec-77, thence to the Nene Valley Railway in 1978 for storage and restoration. TRB 12529 later damaged by fire at Wansford 20-Oct-78 during restoration work, remains stored and sold to Sail & Steam in 1994 for restoration but this organisation went into liquidation and coach remained at Wansford. Residual asbestos removed and coach reduced to an underframe only by Feb-07. This believed cut-up during Nov-10.
3085	Unit withdrawn 13-Mar-71 and initially stored in Wimbledon South Sidings, unit moved to Selhurst for stripping 30-Jun-71. After stripping unit stored at Micheldever and moved for scrapping from there 27-Sep-71 to A King Ltd, Wymondham.

4-COR Units 3101 - 3158

The original 4-COR units were built in two batches, one of twenty-nine units to run with the 4-RES units for the Portsmouth No. 1 extension and a second of twenty-six units to run with the 4-BUF units for the Portsmouth No. 2 extension. Both batches of units were identical and the first completed between February and July 1937; the later batch between January and April 1938 (these having the nearside power jumpers fitted from new).

All units were constructed at Eastleigh works and consisted of two motor brake thirds, a trailer composite and a trailer third. The motor coaches and TCK were identical to those already described in the 4-BUF units.

These units therefore weighed 158¼ tons and seated 30 first and 196 third class passengers. The first class section of the TCK was marshalled at the centre of the unit and the corridor was to the same side as that in the TTK.

Trailer Corridor Thirds

Built to diagram No. 2009, the TTK was to the same internal layout as those in the earlier 6-PAN and 6-PUL sets and had eight full compartments 6' 3" wide and a coupe compartment 4' 4½" wide seating four, linked by a side corridor with a lavatory at each end. It weighed 32 tons 13cwt and seated 68 third (later second) and was marshalled with the coupe compartment against the motor

coach. Accordingly the corridor was on the nearside when the adjacent motor coach was leading. Smoking was allowed in the coupé and three adjacent compartments and also in the three at the other end of the coach.

4 COR units in Service

Routine maintenance was carried out alongside their sister 4-RES and 4-BUF units at Fratton, Wimbledon Park, Streatham Hill and (later) Lovers Walk depots.

Four units were destroyed during the war and were replaced afterwards by new construction, along with a further three units made up from damaged vehicles and new construction to replace the three 4-RES units lost to war damage. The units were numbered 3101 - 3155, with 3156 - 3158 as the extra units formed after the war.

In 1966 an additional ten units were formed using former 4 RES unit motor coaches and former 6-PUL/PAN trailers, numbered 3159 - 3168.

4 COR Liveries

From January 1964, repainted units gained a small yellow warning panel on the corridor end of the cabs, unit 3122 being amongst the first SR units so treated.

Units were repainted into all-over blue livery from June 1966 starting with 3124. The first eleven units (nos. 3103/08/10/14/21/24/32/33/34/47/52) had the intermediate version with blue ends and small panel; all these were

4-COR No. 3111 about to leave London Bridge as the leading set on the 1-24pm to Littlehampton, 9 April 1949. Introduced in February 1937, this set had a working life of 35 years.

J H Aston

painted blue a second time with full yellow ends.

Unit nos. 3109/12/25/27/40 had the yellow area wrap further round onto the bodysides when painted blue.

Unit 3116 received full yellow ends with green livery after collision repairs during 1965; units 3111/23/31/42/49 also carried this scheme.

Unit 3118 was the last to run in all-over green livery in February 1970 and 3116 the last green with yellow ends until November 1970.

4-COR Demise and Withdrawal

Units were displaced off the Mid-Sussex line in January 1964 by 4-CEP and 4-BEP stock, the displaced units seeing more use on other Central Division routes as the Brighton 6 car units began to be withdrawn for disposal. Delivery of new 4-CIG and 4-BIG units for the Portsmouth line saw further units displaced; these being then used on the Reading line from October 1970 and 'Coastway' routes from Brighton (in turn displacing 2-BIL and 2-HAL stock for withdrawal).

Subsequent batches of 4-CIG and 4-VEP units were then ordered to allow replacement of the 4-COR units themselves, their last 'Main Line' duties following timetable changes from 1st May 1971 being a few trips on the Brighton line:

06.45 West Worthing to Victoria.
08.03 Hove to London Bridge.
09.28 Victoria to Brighton.
17.41 London Bridge to Littlehampton.

Units began to be withdrawn during the latter part of 1971 following further deliveries of 4-CIG and 4-VEP units and this continued into 1972, with units being removed from Reading line workings from 3rd January 1972. A few 4-VEP units (7825 - 7828) displaced 2-HAP units onto the East Coastway allowing further 4-COR units to be withdrawn from 5th August 1972 and they were only used irregularly on the West Coastway route after this date. The remaining units then surviving on the East Coastway were replaced from 30th September 1972 and three units were retained in working order for a farewell special on 9th December 1972 thence withdrawn.

Formation of 4 COR Units 3101 to 3158

The following table lists new dates (where known), unit formations, post war replacement units and withdrawal dates. Also code for scrap dealer and date (where units disposed of as complete 4-car sets). Electrical codes allocated to each vehicle from about 1963 are also shown.

Unit no. Diag no.	New	MBT 2114	TRB 2009	TCK 2309	MBT 2114	Withdrawn	Scrapped	Notes
Code		A-1A	BB	BA	A			Codes from c.1963
3101	Feb-37	11081	10055	11791	11082 11244	1-Jan-72	May-72 W	
3102	Feb-37	11083	10056	11792	11084	14-Oct-72	May-73 N	
3103	Feb-37	11085	10057	11793	11086	6-May-72	May-73 N	
3104	Feb-37	11087	10058	11794	11088	6-May-72	Nov-72 C	
3105	Feb-37	11089	10059	11795 11751 [3]	11090	8-Apr-72	Nov-72 C	[3] Former 6-PUL TCK, Code BA-1A
3106	Feb-37	11091	10060	11796	11092	6-May-72	Nov-72 C	
3107	Feb-37	11093	10061	11797	11094	1-Jan-72	May-72 W	
3108	Feb-37	11095	10062	11798	11096	14-Oct-72	May-73 W	
3109	Feb-37	11097	10063	11799	11098	14-Oct-72	May-73 W	
3110	Feb-37	11099	10064	11800	11100	11-Sep-71	Jan-72 N (2)	
3111	Feb-37	11101	10065	11801	11102	6-May-72	Nov-72 C	
3112	Feb-37	11103	10066	11802 11839	11104 11216	1-Jan-72	Jul-72 F	
3113	Feb-37	11105	10067	11803	11106	1-Jan-72	May-72 W	
3114	Apr-37	11107	10068	11804	11108	6-May-72	Nov-72 C	
3115	Apr-37	11109	10069	11805	11110	1-Jan-72	Jun-72 W	
3116	Apr-37	11111 11147 11211	10070	11806	11112 11150	16-Dec-72	Feb-73 W	
3117	Apr-37	11113	10071	11807	11114	26-Mar-41	P'Hbr	Scrapped Portsmouth Harbour
3117	Nov-46	11118	10071	11809	11114	6-May-72	Jan-73 C	Post-war replacement unit
3118	Apr-37	11115 11133	10072	11808 11765 [4]	11116	5-Aug-72	Feb-73 W	[4] Former 6-PUL TCK, Code BA-1A

Waterloo post-1967. Left is the then current BR styling in the form of 4TC set No 420 ready to be propelled to Bournemouth with the '92' semi-fast service. Right is the same set as was seen on p11, No 3111, still in green but with full yellow end. Ironically the newer TC set is not, for the present at least, required to have this embellishment.

3119	Apr-37	11117	10073	11809	11118	26-Mar-41	P'Hbr	Scrapped Portsmouth Harbour
3119	Nov-46	11117	10073	11859	11192	6-May-72	May-73 C	Post-war replacement unit
3120	Apr-37	11119	10074	11810	11120	6-May-72	Nov-72 C	
3121	Apr-37	11121 11230	10075	11811	11122 11148	9-Oct-71	Feb-72 B	
3122	Apr-37	11123	10076	11812	11124	5-Aug-72	Jul-73 W	
3123	Apr-37	11125	10077	11813 11819 11813	11126 11138 11126	16-Dec-72	Feb-73 W	
3124	Apr-37	11127	10078	11814	11128 11034 [5] 11128	9-Oct-71	Feb-72 B	[5] Former 6-PUL MBS
3125	Jul-37	11129	10079	11815	11130	1-Jan-72	See notes	
3126	Jul-37	11131	10080	11816	11132	1-Jan-72	Jul-72 F	
3127	Jul-37	11133 11194	10081	11817	11134	28-Feb-70	Jun-70 N (2)	
3128	Jul-37	11135	10082	11818	11136	14 Oct-72	May-73 W	
3129	Jul-37	11137	10083	11819 11813 11819	11138 11126 11138	6-May-72	Jan-73 C	
3130	1-38	11178	10084	11820	11177 11139	6-May-72	See notes	
3131	1-38	11180	10085	11821	11179	14-Oct-72	See notes	
3132	1-38	11182	10086	11822	11181 11181	14-Oct-72	Feb-73 N	

3133	1-38	11184	10087	11823	11183	6-May-72	Jan-73 C	
3134	2-38	11186 11241	10088	11824 11852	11185 11195	1-Jan-72	See notes	
3135	8-Feb-38	11188	10089	11825 11832	11187 11113 11187	23-Sep-72	See notes	
3136	Feb-38	11190	10090	11826	11189	14-Oct-72	Feb-73 W	
3137	Feb-38	11191	10091	11827	11192	4-Sep-40	(3 coaches)	
3137	Jul-46	11113 11187 11113	10091	11827	11108 2	5-Aug-72	Sep-73 W	Post-war replacement unit
3138	Feb-38	11194 11133 11115	10092	11828 11808	11193	1-Jan-72	Jul-72 F	
3139	Feb-38	11196	10093	11829	11195 11185	1-Jan-72	Jul-72 W	
3140	Feb-38	11198	10094	11830	11197	6-May-72	Jan-73 C	
3141	Feb-38	11200	10095	11831	11199	14-Oct-72	Feb-73 N	
3142	3-Mar-38	11202 11161	10096	11832 11825	11201	16-Dec-72	See notes	
3143	Mar-38	11204	10097	11833	11203	14-Oct-72	Feb-73 W	
3144	Mar-38	11205	10098	11834	11206	12-Nov-41	(3 coaches)	
3144	Sep-46	11257	10111	11834	11205 11112	9-Oct-71	Feb-72 B	Post-war replacement unit
3145	Mar-38	11208 11111	10099	11835	11207	14-Oct-72	Feb-73 W	
3146	Mar-38	11210	10100	11836	11209	1-Jan-72	Jul-72 W	
3147	Mar-38	11212 11171	10101	11837	11211 11147	1-Jan-72	Jul-72 F	
3148	Mar-38	11214 11036 6 11214	10102	11838	11213 11208	4-Dec-71	Jun-72 W	6 Former 6-PUL MBS.
3149	Mar-38	11215	10103	11839 11802	11216 11104	1-Jan-72	See notes	
3150	Mar-38	11218 11239	10104	11840	11217	1-Jan-72	Sep-72 F	
3151	Mar-38	11220	10105	11841	11219	5-Aug-72	Jul-73 W	
3152	Mar-38	11222	10106	11842	11221	1-Jan-72	Jul-72 F	
3153	Mar-38	11224	10107	11843	11223	1-Jan-72	Jun-72 W	
3154	Mar-38	11226	10108	11844	11225	14-Oct-72	Jul-73 W	
3155	Mar-38	11228	10109	11845	11227	1-Jan-72	Jun-72 W	
3156	Jul-46	11218	10098	11807	11232	1-Jan-72	Jul-72 F	Post-war 4-RES replacement unit
3157	Oct-46	11151	10112	11860	11152	1-Jan-72	Jul-72 W	Post-war 4-RES replacement unit
3158	Jan-46	11158	10110	11861 11824	11247	6-May-72	See notes	Post-war 4-RES replacement unit

Key letter codes for Scrap Dealers			
B	Bird Group, Long Marston.	N	J. Cashmore Ltd, Newport.
C	G. Cohen Ltd, Morriston.	T	T. J. Thomson, Stockton.
F	T. W. Ward Ltd, Briton Ferry.	W	T. W. Ward Ltd, Beighton.

The old Waterloo and the old era - a generation now past and also decidedly dejected. Parcels on trolleys / all over blue livery and a 4-COR set No 3156 having the full yellow end but also looking decidedly dated. Notice too the luggage lifts and in the distance at the end of the platform, the 'Southern Electric' style cover above the exit gates.

Individual Unit Notes 3101 - 3158	
3101	Unit badly damaged by V1 blast at Wimbledon Park 29-Jun-44 and MBT 11082 withdrawn from 5-Aug-44. Replaced by 11244 (ex 3080) from Dec-44. Underframe of 11082 converted to flat wagon for use in Ashford Works yard, numbered DS 107. A new 11082 built Jul-46 and included in 'new' unit 3137. Possible that underframe of DS107 then used in repair of 11212 in 3147 during 1956. Following withdrawal unit stored initially at Gatwick and moved to Selhurst for stripping 8-Mar-72. Moved for scrapping 13-Apr-72 from Norwood Yard.
3102	Following withdrawal unit stored initially at Ford before moving to Selhurst for stripping 20-Jan-73. After stripping unit moved to Micheldever before moving again (20-Feb-73) for scrapping.
3103	Following withdrawal unit stored initially at Lancing, moving to Gatwick 4-Sep-72 and on to Horsham 22-Sep-72. Unit to Selhurst for stripping c.11-Nov-72 and then hauled to Micheldever 17-Jan-73 for storage before moving again (20-Feb-73) for scrapping.
3104	Unit stored at Lancing from 29-Apr-72 and withdrawn 6-May-72. After stripping at Selhurst unit to Micheldever for storage 5-Aug-72. Moved for scrapping from there 14-Nov-72 to Salisbury, thence to Westbury 16-Nov-72, moving forward to Morriston shortly afterwards.
3104	Unit out of use by 8-Mar-72 and stored at Gatwick, moving to Selhurst for stripping where TCK 11795 exchanged with 11751 (ex 3165). Unit withdrawn 8-Apr-72 and after stripping unit moved to Clapham Junction on 10-May-72 thence on to Micheldever 27-May-72. Unit moved again (21-Nov-72) for scrapping.
3105	TTK 10060 damaged in buffer stop collision at Waterloo 26-Aug-39. Unit stored at Lancing from 29-Apr-72 and withdrawn 6-May-72. After stripping at Selhurst unit to Micheldever for storage 5-Aug-72. Moved (14-Nov-72) for scrapping to Salisbury, thence on to Westbury 16-11-72, moving forward to Morriston shortly afterwards.

3107	Following withdrawal unit stored initially at Gatwick before moving to Selhurst for stripping 8-Mar-72. Moved for scrapping 13-Apr-72 from Norwood Yard.
3108	MBS 11095 experimentally fitted with roller blind route indicators in 1958, the first SR designed vehicle to be so fitted. Following withdrawal unit stored initially at Lancing. After stripping unit moved to Brent Yard 30-Mar-73 and forward for scrapping 7-Apr-73 from there.
3109	Unit stored at Lancing from 29-Sep-72 and withdrawn 14-Oct-72. After stripping unit moved to Brent Yard 30-Mar-73 and forward for scrapping 7-Apr-73 from there.
3110	After stripping unit moved to Wimbledon Park and split-up both trailers moved to Hoo Junction 4-Nov-71 where their bodies were broken-up and underframes used for basis of long-welded-rail carrying wagons, 10064 to DB975526 and 11800 to DB975527; conversion taking place at Stewarts Lane c.Nov-71. Both MBSs moved to Micheldever for storage and moved for scrapping 17-Jan-72 from Basingstoke.
3111	Unit stored at Barnham from 30-Apr-72 and withdrawn 6-May-72. Moved to Selhurst for stripping c.21-Jul-72 thence hauled to Guildford for storage, moving to Woking 4-Oct-72 and on to Micheldever 7-Oct-72. Moved for scrapping 21-Nov-72 from there.
3112	Unit damaged by enemy action (*probably at Fratton depot 12-Jun-41*) with both MBT 11104 and TCK 11802 to 3149 from Dec-41 after repairs. Replaced by 11216 and 11839 (both ex 3149) in Jul-41. Unit to Selhurst 3-Jan-72 for stripping and hauled to Micheldever 28-Mar-72 for storage. Moved for scrapping 17-Jul-72 from there.
3113	Following withdrawal unit stored initially at Gatwick before moving to Selhurst for stripping 4-Apr-72. Moved for scrapping 13-Apr-72 from Norwood Yard.
3114	Unit stored at Lancing from 29-Apr-72 and withdrawn 6-May-72. After stripping at Selhurst unit to Micheldever for storage 5-Aug-72. Moved 14-Nov-72 for scrapping from there to Salisbury thence on to Westbury 16-11-72, moving forward to Morriston shortly afterwards.

Unit 3142 of 1938. Some vehicles from the original 1938 formation were changed over the years (see table on p21), but a 4-COR set with this number is now preserved as the sole representative full set of these once numerous trains. R F Roberts

3115	Following withdrawal unit stored initially at Gatwick before moving to Selhurst for stripping 4-Apr-72 and storage in Norwood Yard. Moved for scrapping 10-Jan-72 from there.
3116	Unit damaged by enemy incendiaries at Fratton Depot 8-Apr-41 and MBT 11112 badly burnt out. MBT 11111 to 3145 c.May-41, 11112 to 3083 Aug-43 after repairs. Replaced by 11147 (ex 3058) Sep-41 and 11150 (ex 3059) May-41. Unit propelled a stores van through buffers and wall at Durnsford Road Jun-65; MBS 11147 damaged and to 3147 from Jan-67 after repairs. Replaced by 11211 (ex 3147) from Jul-65. Unit stored at Lancing from 30-Sept-72 until used for farewell rail tour 9-Dec-72 then to Barnham for store and withdrawn 16-Dec-72. After stripping at Selhurst unit stored at Crystal Palace before moving for scrapping 17-Feb-73 from there.
3117	Unit destroyed at Portsmouth Harbour by enemy incendiaries 10-Jan-41 and all coaches withdrawn 26-Mar-41 when remains were scrapped. Only the underframe of 11114 was salvaged and later cut-up (*probably at Lancing in 1943*). A new replacement unit was built in 1946 as follows: MBT 11113 to new 3137 (Jul-46). TTK 10071 (May-46). TCK 11807 to 'new' 3156 (Jun-46). MBT 11114 (Nov-46). TCK 11809 (Nov-46), original ran in 3119. MBT 11118 (Nov-46), original ran in 3119. TTK 10071 used temporarily in 3074 from May-46 until MBTs for 3117 ready Nov-46. Unit stored at Barnham from 30-Apr-72 and withdrawn 6-May-72. Unit moved to Ford for a while thence to Lancing before working to Selhurst 3-Aug-72 for stripping. Unit then hauled to Micheldever 14-Aug-72 for storage before moving for scrapping 9-Jan-73 from there.
3118	Unit damaged during 1969 (*where?*) and MBS 11115 and TCK 11808 both to 3138. Replaced Feb-70 by 11133 (ex 3127 via 3138) and 11765 (ex 3161). Unit then weighed 161 tons 13cwt. On withdrawal 5-Aug-72 unit to Lancing for initial storage, moving to Gatwick 2-Sep-72 and to Selhurst for stripping 22-Sep-72. Unit hauled to Hither Green for storage 24-Oct-72 before moving for scrapping 7-Feb-73 from there; though train spent a while at Brent Yard (forward from there ?-Feb-73).
3119	Unit destroyed at Portsmouth Harbour by enemy incendiaries 10-Jan-41 and all coaches withdrawn 26-Mar-41 when remains scrapped. (*See illustration overleaf.*) Underframes of 11118 and 11809 salvaged, that of 11118 later cut-up (*probably at Lancing in 1943*), whilst that of 11809 was converted to a flat wagon for use at Lancing Works from Sep-47 being numbered 137 S. This wagon was withdrawn 30-Jun-51 and probably scrapped at Lancing shortly afterwards. A new replacement unit was built in 1946 as follows: MBT 11117 (Nov-46). TTK 10073 (May-46). TCK 11809 to new 3117 (Nov-46). MBT 11118 to new 3117 (Nov-46). TCK 11859 (May-46), new number. MBT 11192 (Nov-46), original ran in 3137. TTK 10073 and TCK 11859 both used temporarily in 6-CITY units 3041 (10073) and 3043 (11859) from May-46 to Nov-46 when MBTs of 3119 was ready. Unit in collision with loco-hauled Set 296 at Waterloo 3-Jun-60 and MBS 11117 badly damaged with half of its side torn away. The remaining three coaches were stored at Micheldever pending repairs to 11117 at Eastleigh. Unit back to traffic Mar-61. Unit stored at Barnham 30-Apr-72 and withdrawn 6-May-72. Unit later moved to Ford thence onto Lancing, Tattenham Corner from 2-Aug-72 and Crystal Palace from 4-Oct-72 prior to stripping at Selhurst. Unit then hauled to Hither Green 6-Jan-73 for storage prior to moving to Micheldever before moving for scrapping 14-May-73 (this move also included the trailers of unit 3164).
3120	Unit stored at Lancing 29-Apr-72 and withdrawn 6-May-72. Unit to Selhurst 3-Aug-72 for stripping and hauled to Micheldever 2-Sep-72 for storage before being moved for scrapping 21-Nov-72 from there.
3121	MBS 11121 temporarily used in 3130 (vice 11139) Aug-58 to Oct-58 (*reason unknown, probable collision*). Unit damaged about Sep-70 (*location unknown*) and MBSs 11121 and 11122 both exchanged with 11230 and 11148 (ex 3073) at Selhurst. Following withdrawal unit stored initially at Lancing. After stripping at Selhurst unit moved for scrapping 16-Feb-73 from Norwood Yard.

3122	On withdrawal 5-Aug-72 unit to Lancing for initial storage before moving to Fratton 30-Aug-72 for use in accident exercise 3-Sep-72. Unit moved to Chichester 15-Nov-72 thence to Selhurst for stripping 6-Jan-73. Unit hauled to Micheldever 17-Jan-73 for storage before moving for scrapping 14-May-73 from there.
3123	MBS 11126 and TCK 11813 damaged at Streatham Hill 16-Dec-47 and exchanged with 11138 and 11819 (both ex 3129) 3-48 for a period (*date of reversion unknown*). Unit stored at Lancing from 30-Sep-72 until used for farewell rail tour 9-Dec-72 thence to Barnham for store and withdrawal 16-Dec-72. After stripping at Selhurst unit stored at Crystal Palace before moving for scrapping 17-Feb-73 from there.
3124	MBS 11128 to 4 PUL 3059 from Jul-64 and replaced by 6-PUL MBS 11034 (ex 3017). Unit then ran permanently coupled to unit 3148 (which had been similarly treated) as a fixed eight-car train seating 60 first and 392 second. This eight-car train was 533' 10" long and weighed 341½ tons. Unit reverted to original formation Jun-65. Following withdrawal unit stored initially at Lancing prior to stripping at Selhurst before moving for scrapping 23-Feb-72 from Norwood Yard.
3125	Unit withdrawn 1-Jan-72 and to Selhurst for stripping. Unit hauled to Hoo Junction by 17-Feb-72 and MBS 11129 scrapped there by 11-Mar-74. Bodies of both trailers also broken-up there and their underframes used for basis of long-welded-rail carrying wagons, TSK 10079 to DB975529 and TCK 11815 to DB975530; conversion taking place at Stewarts Lane c.Feb-72. MBS 11130 stored at Hoo Junction body. Broken up c.Dec-76 and underframe scrapped there Feb-77.
3126	Unit to Selhurst for stripping 3-Jan-72 thence hauled to Micheldever for storage 29-Feb-72. Moved for scrapping 30-May-72 though not cut-up until Jul-72.

A damaged 4 COR set being pulled through Fratton station en-route to the nearby depot and assessment following enemy damage at Portsmouth Harbour. Not surprisingly the remnant of the carriage bodies on the three vehicles seen burnt-out were condemned, although the underframes were re-used.

3127	Unit damaged in side-scrape at Wimbledon Park 23-Jun-69 (with only MBS 11133 undamaged) and stored at Micheldever. 11133 exchanged with damaged 11194 (ex 3138) Jan-70 and unit withdrawn 28-Feb-70 before being used for a number of civil defence exercises including one at Woking 15-Mar-70. Both MBSs 11134 and 11194 moved Selhurst to Micheldever 8-Apr-70 and scrapped by J Cashmore Ltd, Newport having moved from Micheldever 28-May-70. Both trailers moved to Woking thence onto Hoo Junction c.21-Mar-70 where both bodies broken-up and their underframes used for basis of long-welded-rail carrying wagons; TSK 10081 to DB975519 from 16-Oct-71 and TCK 11817 to DB975524 from 25-Mar-72 (conversion taking place at Stewarts Lane).
3128	MBT 11135 and TTK 10082 both temporarily replaced by 6-PAN MBT 11073 and TTK 10040 (ex 3030) during 1944 following enemy action damage. Unit weighed 169½ tons for duration of this change. Following withdrawal unit stored initially at Lancing. After stripping unit moved to Brent Yard 30-Mar-73 moving forward for scrapping 7-Apr-73 from there.
3129	MBS 11137 and TSK 10083 damaged at Wimbledon 28-Feb-48 and MBS 11138 and TCK 11819 both exchanged with damaged 11126 and 11813 (both ex 3123) in Mar-48 for a period whilst all coaches repaired, (*date of reversion unknown*). Unit stored briefly at Three Bridges from 22-Apr-72 before moving to Barnham 30-Apr-72 and withdrawal 6-May-72. Unit to Selhurst c.21-Jul-72 for stripping before being hauled to Micheldever 2-Sep-72 for storage. Moved for scrapping 9-Jan-73 from there.
3130	MBT 11177 exchanged with 11139 (ex 3054) from Dec-45 following enemy action damage (*details, date and location unknown*). MBS 11139 temporarily replaced by 11121 (ex 3121) Aug-58 to Oct-58 (*reason unknown, probable collision*). Unit withdrawn 6-May-72 being initially stored at Lancing thence Ford before moving to Tattenham Corner 2-Aug-72 and on to Crystal Palace 4-Oct-72. Unit then to Hither Green 6-Jan-73 but both MBSs 11139 and 11178 moved to Selhurst and held for possible use as Instruction Train (but not so used). After stripping hauled to Micheldever 4-Dec-73 and moved for scrapping 28-Feb-74 to T. W. Ward Ltd, Beighton. Both trailers TSK 10084 and TCK 11820 scrapped by G Cohen Ltd, Morriston 4-Feb-74 from Micheldever.
3131	MBS 11180 damaged at Wimbledon c.Aug-57 (*details unknown*). Unit withdrawn 14-Oct-72 and MBS 11179 claimed as part of the National Collection by the NRM and moved for store at Preston Park immediately on withdrawal. Remaining three coaches stored in Brighton Top Yard until moved to Chichester 10-Mar-73 for an accident exercise. These then moved to Selhurst for stripping 28-Apr-73 and sent for scrapping, moving from Brent Yard to T. W. Ward Ltd, Beighton c.2-Jun-73. MBS 11179 taken from Preston Park to York for restoration 3-Dec-77.
3132	Unit damaged by enemy incendiaries at Portsmouth Harbour 10-Jan-41 and MBT 11181 withdrawn 26-Mar-41 (fell into harbour and not retrieved until 1946). Remaining three coaches marooned on pier for duration, eventually moving to Lancing for overhaul c.Oct-46. A replacement 11181 built about Oct-46 and to Lancing to be formed with the three repaired coaches. Following withdrawal, unit stored initially at Lancing, moving to Crystal Palace by Nov-72 thence to Selhurst for stripping 12-Jan-73, returned to Crystal Palace before moving to Basingstoke 25-Jan-73 and on for scrapping 26-Jan-73.
3133	Unit stored at Lancing 29-Apr-72 and withdrawn 6-May-72. After stripping at Selhurst unit hauled to Hither Green 24-Oct-72, moving to Micheldever 25-Nov-72 for storage. Moved for scrapping 23-Jan-73 from there.
3134	Unit damaged by enemy bombing at Victoria 9-Oct-40 but repaired. Unit in collision with 3139 at Drayton Crossing 8-Feb-63 and MBS 11186 severely damaged and cut-up on site. MBS 11185 to 3139 and TCK 11824 to 3158 from Mar-64. Replaced by damaged MBS 11195 (ex 3139) and after repairs unit back to traffic Apr-64 with TCK 12852 and MBS 11241 (both ex 3079). Unit in collision with 7807 at Fratton Depot 30-Dec-71 and withdrawn 1-Jan-72 and MBS 11241 and TCK 11852 both scrapped at Fratton by 22-Apr-72. TSK 10088 moved to Eastleigh 12-Jan-72 and became internal-user vehicle IU 083145 from 21-May-73 at Eastleigh Works. Following fire damage in Jul-78 the body was broken-up 9-May-79 and underframe retained as a 'flat', believed cut-up during 1988. MBS 11195 retained at Fratton for possible preservation in the Portsmouth area though this did not take place and the coach was sent to Chichester 15-Nov-72 before moving to Selhurst for stripping 6-Jan-73. Coach then hauled to Micheldever for storage 17-Jan-73 and on to Eastleigh by May-73. Moved to Bird, Long Marston for scrapping 17-May-73.

Set 3135 at London Bridge.

3135	Unit new into traffic 8-Feb-38. MBS 11187 damaged in collision at with 2059 and 3076 at Wimbledon Park 20-Jun-66 and temporarily exchanged with 11113 (ex 3137) 28-Jul-66. Reverted to original formation in Dec-66. Unit stored at Lancing 20-Sep-72 and withdrawn 23-Sep-72. Unit to Selhurst for stripping 28-Apr-73 and MBS 11187 and TCK 11825 both sold for preservation, MBS 11187 for private preservation and moved to Cheshunt by 11-May-73, TCK 11825 reformed into unit 3142 6-May-73, this unit being purchased by the Southern Electric Group. Other two coaches (MBS 11188 and TSK 10089) sent for scrapping, moving from Brent Yard to T. W. Ward Ltd, Beighton c.2-Jun-73. MBS 11187 later donated to the Southern Electric Group for preservation alongside unit 3142 and moved to the Nene Valley Railway at Wansford by May-84, later by road to St Leonards Railway Depot c.1993. Coach subsequently moved by road to the LT museum site at Acton 6-Dec-05.
3136	Following withdrawal unit stored initially at Ford before moving to Selhurst 18-Oct-72 for stripping, thence hauled to Hither Green 30-Oct-72 for storage. Moved for scrapping 7-Feb-73 from there, though train spent a while at Brent Yard (moving forward from there ?-2-73).

3137	Unit badly damaged by enemy action at Portsmouth Harbour 12-Aug-40 with three coaches burnt-out and withdrawn 4-Sep-40; underframes being cut-up during 1943 at Lancing (11192 on 23-Jun-43, 10091 on 8-Sep-43 and that of 11827 unknown). MBT 11191 to 3083 from Aug-43 after repairs.
	A new replacement unit built in 1946 as follows, this being the first of the 'replacement' units into traffic in Aug-46:
	                  MBT 11113 (Jul-46), original ran in 3117.
	                  TTK 10091 (Jul-46).
	                  TCK 11827 (Jun-46).
	                  MBT 11082 (Jul-46), original ran in 3101.
	                  MBT 11192 (Nov-46) to 'new' 3119.
	MBS 11082 and TCK 11827 damaged in collision with van train at Fratton 30-Jul-66. 10091 and 11113 spare whilst repairs completed, though MBS 11113 temporarily exchanged with damaged 11187 (ex 3135) 28-Jul-66 until Dec-66.
	On withdrawal unit stored initially at Lancing before moving to Gatwick 2-Sep-72 thence on to Selhurst for stripping 28-Sep-72. After stripping unit hauled to Crystal Palace 4-Oct-72 thence to Hither Green 6-Jan-73; moving for scrapping 1-Aug-73 from there.

3138	TCK 11828 removed from unit c.Jan-62 to 3056 (running as a 3-car); 3138 also ran as 3-car (usually coupled to 3056). TCK 11828 returned to unit c.Nov-62. Unit damaged in collision with 5357 at Streatham Hill 24-Dec-69 and withdrawn 28-Feb-70. Damaged MBS 11194 exchanged with 11133 (ex 3127). Damaged 11828 to 3161 and replaced with 11808 (ex 3118). MBS 11133 then exchanged with 11115 (ex 3118) Feb-70 and unit reinstated 6-Mar-70. Following withdrawal unit stored initially at Gatwick before moving to Selhurst for stripping 8-Mar-72. Unit hauled to Woking 29-Mar-72 thence onto Micheldever 15-Apr-72 before moving for scrapping 27-Jun-72 from there.
3139	Unit in collision with 3134 at Drayton Crossing 8-Feb-63; MBS 11195 severely damaged and placed into 3134 after repairs. Replaced by MBS 11185 (ex 3134). On withdrawal unit to Selhurst for stripping and hauled to Micheldever 28-Feb-72 for storage before moving for scrapping 28-Jun-72 from there, though train delayed for 10 days at Old Kew Sidings.
3140	Unit stored at Lancing from 29-Apr-72 before withdrawal 6-May-72, moving to Gatwick 4-Sep-72. Unit hauled to Horsham for further storage 22-Sep-72 thence to Selhurst for stripping c.11-Nov-72. Unit hauled to Micheldever for storage 4-Dec-72 before moving for scrapping 23-Jan-73 from there.
3141	One MBS (*which?*) side damaged (*location unknown*) Nov-61 and repaired at Lancing Jan-62. Following withdrawal unit stored initially at Lancing, moving to Crystal Palace by Nov-72 thence onto Selhurst for stripping 12-Jan-73 before returning to Crystal Palace. Moved to Basingstoke 25-Jan-73 and on for scrapping 26-Jan-73.
3142	Unit new into traffic 3-3-38. Unit damaged in collision with 2-BIL 2045 at Denville Jct. Havant 17-Jun-39 but repaired. Unit damaged in collision with 3065 at Wimbledon Park Jan-45 and MBT 11202 to 3065 after repairs. Replaced by 11161 (ex 3065) from 14-Jun-45. Unit stored at Lancing from 30-Sep-72 until used for farewell rail tour 9-Dec-72 thence to Barnham for store and withdrawal 16-Dec-72. Unit to Selhurst for stripping 28-Apr-73 and TCK 11832 (which had been slightly damaged by fire Jan-73 whilst unit stored at Barnham) was exchanged with 11825 (ex 3135) 6-May-73 prior to sale of unit for preservation. TCK 11832 sent for scrapping, moving from Brent Yard to T. W. Ward Ltd, Beighton c.2-Jun-73. Reformed unit 3142 then hauled from Selhurst to the Ashford Steam Centre 26-May-73 where some restoration undertaken. Unit subsequently moved from Ashford to the Nene Valley Railway 27/28-Feb-76 where unit used in passenger service steam-hauled. Unit then moved to Preston Park 5-Sep-86 for storage and further restoration, moving again to St Leonards Railway Depot 29-Jun-91. Some restoration work was carried out whilst it was there, but the unit was again moved; three coaches moving by road to the 'Woodpax' site adjacent to Sheffield Park station (11161 moving 9/10-Feb-04, 11825 on 11-Feb-04 and 10096 on 12-Feb-04). All three were stored there under tarpaulins awaiting movement to a more suitable site for further restoration. MBS 11201 remained at St Leonards Railway Depot where it was externally restored and part of the interior stripped to show the coach construction for exhibition purposes. The coach was then moved by road to Sheffield Park 18-Jan-05 where it was steam-hauled to Horsted Keynes 20-Jan-05 and berthed in the station as a semi-permanent exhibition coach, opening to the public from 22-Jan-05. The three coaches at Sheffield Park moved by road to the East Kent Railway at Shepherds Well in May-06 (11161 on 22-May-06, 10096 on 23-May-06 and 11825 on 24-May-06) with each being unloaded the following morning.
3143	Unit damaged late 1960 (*possibly in collision with 4-SUB 4108 at Wimbledon Park 28-Dec-60*) and MBS 11203 slightly damaged. Repaired at Eastleigh. Following withdrawal unit stored initially at Ford thence to Selhurst for stripping 20-Jan-73. After stripping unit hauled to Crystal Palace Feb-73 before moving for scrapping 17-Feb-73 from there.

3144	Unit badly damaged by enemy bombing at Fratton Depot 27-Apr-41 and three coaches burnt out. MBT 11206 to 3082, other three coaches withdrawn 12-Nov-41 when remains scrapped. A new replacement unit built in 1946 as follows:
	        MBT 11205 (Sep-46).
	        TTK 10098 (Jun-46) to 'new' 3156.
	        TCK 11834 (Jun-46).
	        MBT 11157 (Sep-46), original ran in 4-RES 3063.
	        TTK 10111 (Sep-46), new number (built to replace restaurant car 12617 of 4 RES 3063).
	Underframes of damaged original coaches 10098 and 11834 both used as basis of Precast Signal Unit carrying wagons based at Exmouth Junction Concrete Works and renumbered 1902S and 1903S respectively. Both these vehicles transferred to WR stock from 23-Mar-63 (*disposal details unknown*).
	Unit ran as 4-BUF in May-57 with TRB 12519 (ex 3073).
	Unit became divided between Clandon and London Road, Guildford 4-Apr-71 tearing out end of MBS 11205, this vehicle then exchanged with 11112 (ex withdrawn 3083) from c.12-Jun-71. Following withdrawal unit stored initially at Lancing prior to stripping at Selhurst. Moved for scrapping 23-Feb-72 from Norwood Yard.

3145	Unit damaged by enemy bombing at Bognor 11-4-41 and MBT 11208 to 3148 after repairs. Replaced by 11111 (ex 3116). Following withdrawal unit stored initially at Ford, moving to Selhurst 18-10-72 for stripping, then hauled to Hither Green 30-10-72 for storage and moved for scrapping 7-2-73 from there, though train spent a while at Brent Yard, forward from there ?-2-73.
3146	The driving cab on one MBS (*which?*) was damaged when unit in collision with vans at Woking 3-Apr-68. Following withdrawal unit stored initially at Gatwick before moving to Selhurst for stripping c.10-Mar-72 thence storage in Norwood Yard. Moved for scrapping 10-Jun-72 from there.
3147	Unit damaged at Woking 23-Dec-55 when hit by steam train hauled by 32327. MBT 11212 repaired at Lancing using underframe of withdrawn 11082 (ex 3101 which had been withdrawn after war damage and converted to a flat numbered DS107). Original underframe of 11212 later cut-up at Eastleigh. MBS 11212 damaged beyond repair in collision at Brighton 7-Apr-65 although not withdrawn until 6-Jul-68 after storage at Micheldever (*disposal unknown, probably broken-up on site*). MBS 11211 to 3116 from Jul-65 and trailers remained stored at Micheldever. Unit returned to traffic Jan-67 in blue with yellow end livery with MBS 11147 (ex 3116 after collision repairs) and MBS 11171 (ex disbanded 4-COR[N] 3070). On withdrawal unit to Selhurst for stripping and hauled to Micheldever 29-Feb-72 for storage. Moved for scrapping 27-Jun-72 from there.
3148	Unit damaged by enemy action (*date and location unknown*) and MBT 11213 to 3074 after repairs. Replaced by 11208 (ex 3145). In Jul-64 MBS 11214 to 4-PUL 3056 and replaced by 6 PUL MBS 11036 (ex 3018) from Oct-64. Unit then ran permanently coupled to unit 3124 (which had been similarly treated) as a fixed eight-car train seating 60 first and 392 second. This eight-car train was 533' 10" long and weighed 341½ tons. Unit reverted to original formation from Jun-65. Following withdrawal unit stored initially at Gatwick before moving to Selhurst 5-5-72 for stripping. Unit moved for scrapping 24-Jun-72 from Norwood Yard.
3149	Unit damaged by enemy action (*probably at Fratton depot 12-6-41*) and MBT 11216 and TCK 11839 to 3112 Jul-41. Replaced from Dec-41 by MBS 11104 and TCK 11802 (both ex 3112 after damage repairs). Upon withdrawal unit to Selhurst for stripping before moving to Beddington Engineers Yard 4-Feb-72. Both MBSs 11104 and 11215 scrapped there by 11-Nov-72 using New Cross Gate staff (along with the bodies of both trailers). Both trailer underframes moved to New Cross Gate 23-Mar-72 for use as the basis of long-welded -rail carrying wagons, TSK 10103 to DB975532 from 9-Sep-72 and TCK 11802 to DB975531 from 19-Aug-72 (conversion taking place at Stewarts Lane).
3150	Unit damaged by enemy action (*date and location unknown*) and MBT 11218 to 'new' 3156 from Jul-46 after repairs. Replaced by 11239 (ex 3078) from Apr-45. Unit withdrawn 1-Jan-72 following collision with 4-CIG 7391 at Farnham 28-Dec-71. Unit hauled to Selhurst 5-Feb-72 for stripping thence to Micheldever c.12-Jun-72 for storage. Moved for scrapping 4-Jul-72, though train recessed en route and still at Margam Yard 4-Sep-72.
3151	Upon withdrawal unit stored initially at Lancing before moving to Selhurst for stripping. Unit then hauled to Guildford thence Woking 4-Oct-72 and on to Micheldever 7-Oct-72 before moving for scrapping 14-May-73 from there.
3152	Unit damaged in buckled rail derailment on the Quarry line at Merstham 27-Jun-49. Unit to Selhurst for stripping 3-Jan-72 and hauled to Micheldever for storage 29-2-72. Moved for scrapping 30-May-72 though not cut-up until Jul-72.
3153	Upon withdrawal unit stored initially at Lancing before moving to Selhurst 25-Apr-72 for stripping. Unit stored in Norwood Yard and moved for scrapping 10-Jun-72 from there.
3154	Unit damaged at Waterloo 10-Jun-47 when hit by misrouted steam train hauled by 21C8 (unit repaired). Unit stored at Lancing from 20-Sep-72 and withdrawn 14-Oct-72. Moved to Selhurst c.28-Apr-73 for stripping and sent for scrapping, moving from Brent Yard c.2-Jun-73.
3155	Following withdrawal, unit initially stored at Gatwick, moving to Selhurst for stripping 4-Apr-72. Unit sent for scrapping 24-Jun-72 from Norwood Yard.

3156	Replacement for withdrawn 4 RES 3058.
	Unit into service Jul-46 using two MBTs ex war damage repairs and two new trailers built Jun-46 as follows:
	MBT 11218 (ex 3150).
	TTK 10098, original had run in 3144.
	TCK 11807, original had run in 3117.
	MBT 11232 (ex 3074).
	Unit to Selhurst 3-Jan-72 for stripping thence hauled to Micheldever 28-Mar-72 for storage. Moved for scrapping 17-Jul-72 from there.
3157	Replacement for withdrawn 4 RES 3060.
	Unit into service Oct-46 using four new vehicles as follows:
	MBT 11151 (Oct-46), original had run in 4-RES 3060.
	TTK 10112 (Sep-46), new number built to replace TRT 12615 of 3060.
	TCK 11860 (Jun-46), new number built to replace TFK 12234 of 3058.
	MBT 11152 (Oct-46), original had run in 4-RES 3060.
	11860 built as 4 RES TFK 12234 but renumbered 11860 prior to use in 3157. This coach initially seated 30 first and 16 third (in the former first class dining saloon now altered to seat one and three aside each side of the off-centre gangway); coach weighed 33 tons, giving 3157 a non-standard seating capacity of 30 first and 188 third and overall weight of 158¾ tons. 11860 later altered to a standard TCK internal layout and unit to standard seating capacity and weight.
	Upon withdrawal unit to Selhurst for stripping thence hauled to Micheldever 28-Feb-72 for storage and moved for scrapping 28-Jun-72 from there, although train delayed for 10 days at Old Kew Sidings.
3158	Replacement for withdrawn 4 RES 3063.
	Unit into service Jan-46 using two MBTs and TCK (rebuilt ex TFK) ex war damage repairs and a new TTK built Jan-46 as follows:
	MBT 11158 (ex 4-RES 3063).
	TTK 10110 (Jan-46), new number built to replace TRT 12606 of 4-RES 3058.
	TCK 11861 rebuilt May-45 from TFK 12232 (ex 4-RES 3063).
	MBT 11247 (ex 4-BUF 3082).
	TCK 11861 seated 30 first and 16 third (in the former first class dining saloon now altered to seat one and three aside each side of the off-centre gangway); coach weighed 33 tons, giving 3158 a non-standard seating capacity of 30 first and 188 third and overall weight of 158¾ tons.
	TCK 11861 withdrawn Mar-64 and replaced by 11824 (ex 3134) so unit to standard capacity and weight. 11861 to Micheldever Mar-64 and later to internal user stock - used as office at Brockenhurst from Jun-66, though moved back to Micheldever for storage by May-67 until condemned 21-Oct-67. Moved to Ashford 4-Oct-68 where body cut-up and underframe converted to Crane Runner DS70280 in 1970.
	Unit stored at Lancing from 29-Apr-72 and withdrawn 6-May-72. Moved to Selhurst 18-Sep-72 for stripping, thence to Hither Green for storage. Both MBSs 11247 and 11158 back at Selhurst by Sep-73 and held for possible use as Instruction Train (but not so used). After stripping to Micheldever 4-Dec-73 thence moved for scrapping by T. W. Ward Ltd, Beighton 28-Feb-74. TSK 10110 and TCK 11824 both scrapped by G Cohen Ltd, Morriston (4-Feb-74 from Micheldever).

4-COR Units 3159 - 3168

The hybrid 4-PUL and 4-COR(N) units formed in January 1964 were obviously only a temporary measure to overcome stock shortages during the delivery of new 4-CIG and 4-BIG stock and by 1965 sufficient numbers of the new units had entered service to enable them to be replaced. This allowed the withdrawal of the remaining 6-PUL and 6-PAN units releasing further trailer vehicles which would allow the 4-PUL and 4-COR(N) units to be reformed as standard 4-COR units.

Of the five 4-PUL sets, two were disbanded and one MBS from each used with two ex 6-PUL trailers to form 'new' unit 3160; the remaining three units had both their existing trailers withdrawn and replaced by ex 6-PUL and 6-PAN trailers.

One of the 4-COR(N) units was also disbanded and the other six had their former 4-RES dining firsts withdrawn and each replaced by a former 6-PUL TCK. These ten 'new' units were classified as 4-COR and renumbered during overhaul at Eastleigh works to continue on from the original number series as units 3159 - 3168.

The internal layout was identical to the original 4 COR units but the former 6-PUL and 6-PAN vehicles had a number of detail differences from the true 4 COR trailers. They were also heavier at 35 tons (6-PUL TSK), 36 tons (6-PUL TCK) or lighter at 31½ tons (6-PAN TSK) each whereas the 4-COR trailers weighed 32¾ tons (TSK) and 32½ tons (TCK). The overall weight of 3159 - 3168 was therefore increased to 160½ tons though 3160 and 3161 which both included two former 6-PUL vehicles were heavier at 164 tons.

The most obvious external difference with these trailers were the ventilation louvres above the door droplights, all original 4 COR/RES/BUF vehicles not having these from new. Former 6 PUL trailers had the unusual double-opening sliding doors between the corridor and compartments and the former 6 PAN trailers had the tall 'dummy' window arrangement opposite alternate compartments.

The electrical codes and diagram numbers for the former 6 PUL/PAN codes were also different; TCKs being to diagram No. 2309, code BA-1A, TSKs being to diagram No. 2010, code BB-1A.

When formed units were in green livery with small yellow panels; all later being repainted blue with full yellow ends.

Formation of 4 COR Units 3159 to 3168

The following table lists 'formed' dates when units were released from C1 overhaul at Eastleigh, unit formations, and withdrawal dates. Also code for scrap dealer and date (where units disposed of as complete 4 car sets). Electrical codes allocated to each vehicle from about 1963 are also shown.

Unit no. Diag no.	New	MBT 2114	TTK 2010	TCK 2307	MBT 2114	Withdrawn	Scrapped	Notes
Code		A-1A	BB-1A	BA-1A	A			Codes from c.1963
3159	15-Oct-65	11159 (3068)	10045 (3068)	11773 (3018)	11160 (3068)	5-Aug-72	Sep-73 W (2)	
3160	22-Oct-65	11149 (3059)	10007 (3016)	11764 (3016)	11153 (3056)	1-Jan-72	Jul-72 F	
3161	8-Jun-66	11177 (3054) 11140	10003 (3003)	11765 (3005) 11828 [7]	11140 (3054) 11246	9-Oct-71	Feb-72 B	[7] Standard 4-COR TCK, Diagram 2309, Code BA.
3162	17-Jun-66	11142 (3055)	10053 (3037)	11755 (3003)	11141 (3055)	9-Oct-71	Feb-72 B	
3163	24-Jun-66	11145 (3057) 11249	10054 (3037)	11788 (3008)	11146 (3057)	6-May-72	Jan-73 C	
3164	6-May-66	11155 (3065)	10034 (3065)	11787 (3008)	11156 (3065)	6-May-72	See notes	
3165	17-Jun-66	11163 (3066)	10033 (3066)	11752 (3013) 11751 11795 [8]	11164 (3066)	6-May-72	Jan-73 C	[8] Standard 4-COR TCK, Diagram 2309, Code BA.
3166	6-May-66	11165 (3067)	10046 (3067)	11751 (3013) 11752	11166 (3067)	9-Oct-71	Feb-72 B	
3167	15-Jun-66	11169 (3069)	10042 (3069)	11784 (3001)	11170 (3069)	1-Jan-72	Sep-72 F	
3168	22-Jul-66	11173 (3071)	10044 (3071)	11776 (3007)	11174 (3071)	1-Jan-72	Jul-72 W	

Key letter codes for Scrap Dealers			
B	Bird Group, Long Marston.	N	J. Cashmore Ltd, Newport.
C	G. Cohen Ltd, Morriston.	T	T. J. Thomson, Stockton.
F	T. W. Ward Ltd, Briton Ferry.	W	T. W. Ward Ltd, Beighton.

	Individual Unit Notes 3159 - 3168
3159	MBS 11159 damaged in derailment at Brighton (Lovers Walk) 25-JUL-72 with unit moved to Lancing for storage and withdrawn 5-Aug-72 thence to Selhurst for stripping. MBSs moved to Hither Green 24-Oct-72 thence to Brent Yard 1-Aug-73 en-route for scrapping by T. W. Ward Ltd, Beighton Sep-73. TSK 10045 later scrapped by A King, Snailwell, moving from Derby 22-May-75. TCK 11773 sold for preservation and TSK 10045 sent from Selhurst to Derby RTC 31-Oct-72 for use as an 'Air Brake test coach' at Derby Research Centre (replacing 2 BIL 2037) though not renumbered into the departmental series. TCK 11773 subsequently moved to the Ashford Steam Centre 8-Dec-72 thence to the Nene Valley Railway along with other 4-COR vehicles from the preserved unit 3142. However, coach then moved by rail to the Swindon & Cricklade Railway, arriving there in May-84 (noted at Swindon 5-May-84). Now in very poor condition moved by road to the Swanage Railway and eventually scrapped at there during May-97. The bogies and buffers were recovered and taken to St Leonards Railway Depot in Jan-02 for use as spares on preserved '3142'.
3160	Unit included two ex 6 PUL trailers and weighed 164 tons. On withdrawal unit to Selhurst for stripping and hauled to Micheldever 29-Feb-72 for storage. Moved for scrapping 27-Jun-72 from there.
3161	Unit included two ex 6 PUL trailers and weighed 164 tons. Unit in collision with 4 BUF 3081 at Wimbledon Park late 1968 and MBS 11140 damaged. 11177 exchanged with damaged 11246 (ex 3081), both then repaired during 1969. TCK 11765 to 3118 Jul-69 and replaced by damaged 11828 (ex 3138); this coach repaired and unit back to traffic formed of 11140 + 10003 + 11828 + 11246; now weighing 160½ tons. Following withdrawal unit stored initially at Lancing before moving to Selhurst for stripping. Moved for scrapping 16-Feb-72 from Norwood Yard.
3162	Following withdrawal unit initially stored at Lancing. After stripping *(at Selhurst?)* unit moved for scrapping 23-Feb-72 from Norwood Yard.
3163	MBS 11145 defective c.Aug-70 and exchanged with 11249 ex withdrawn 4-BUF 3078. Unit stored at Lancing from 29-Apr-72 and withdrawn 6-May-72, moving to Gatwick 4-Sep-72. Unit hauled to Horsham for further storage 22-Sep-72 thence to Selhurst for stripping c.11-Nov-72. Unit hauled to Micheldever for storage 4-Dec-72 and moved for scrapping 23-Jan-73 from there.
3164	Upon withdrawal unit to Selhurst for stripping, hauled to Clapham Junction 10-May-72 and on to Micheldever 27-May-72. Both MBSs 11155 and 11156 moved for scrapping 22-Feb-73 to J Cashmore Ltd, Newport, TSK 10034 and TCK 11787 moved for scrapping 14-May-73 to G Cohen Ltd, Morriston formed into unit 3119 as 6-car for the move.
3165	TCK 11752 exchanged with 11751 (ex 3166) Jul-69. 11751 defective and exchanged with 11795 (ex withdrawn 3105) c.Mar-72 and unit now weighed 157 tons. Unit stored at Barnham from 30-4-72 and withdrawn 6-May-72 and moved to Selhurst for stripping c.21-Jul-72. Hauled to Micheldever 2-Sep-72 and moved for scrapping 9-Jan-73 from there.
3166	TCK 11751 exchanged with 11752 (ex 3165) Jul-69. Following withdrawal unit initially stored at Lancing before moving to Selhurst for stripping. Moved for scrapping 16-Feb-72 from Norwood Yard.
3167	Unit to Selhurst 3-Jan-72 for stripping thence hauled to Micheldever 28-Mar-72 for storage. Moved for scrapping 17-Jul-72 from there (although unit still in Margam Yard 4-Sep-72).
3168	Upon withdrawal unit to Selhurst for stripping thence hauled to Micheldever 28-Feb-72 for storage; moving for scrapping 28-Jun-72 from there (although train delayed for 10 days at Old Kew Sidings).

4-GRI Units 3086 - 3088

Three 4 RES units 3056/65/68 had their kitchen seconds extensively rebuilt from April 1961 as griddle cars similar to the vehicles in the new Clacton line units which were being introduced at this time. The rebuilt coaches consisted of a short central gangway separating a staff lavatory and storage cupboard which led into the buffet saloon with seating for 12 at four tables, those to one side of the gangway having four seats, those to the other only two.

There was an emergency unglazed door located between the two four-seat tables and a service door on the opposite side of the coach directly opposite the buffet counter. Then followed the buffet and kitchen area with the buffet counter at the saloon end, the kitchen in the middle of the vehicle and a small bar facing onto a bar saloon with seating for 14 arranged in small bays around the perimeter and another short centre gangway separating two storage areas.

There were two public access doors along this corridor one opposite the kitchen, the other by the bar area. There was one public door on the other side of the coach by the bar counter and a further service door was provided directly into the rear of the kitchen area, giving a total of three along each side of the coach (of which only two were available to passengers on one side and one the other).

These 26 seats were unclassified and the modified vehicles weighed 34 tons reducing the overall unit weight to 160 tons.

The former dining saloon in the trailer first was now regarded as ordinary first class seating when there was no buffet service, so this coach now seated 42 first and the unit total was therefore altered to 42 first, 104 second and 26 unclassified in the griddle car.

These vehicles were allocated electrical codings from about 1963 and the revised diagram number of the griddle car was 2572.

After rebuilding, the griddle cars did not return to their original unit and they included many BR standard fittings including new double-glazed windows (three on the corridor and one on the kitchen side being of shallower depth than usual) and at the time of withdrawal (20th November 1971) were effectively less than ten years old.

The units re-entered service in their new forms as follows:

3068 Jan-62,

3065 Apr-62 (newly converted griddle car ran briefly in 3069 from c.Feb-62 to Apr-62),

3056 Nov-62.

When the remaining 4 RES units were converted to 4-PUL or 4 COR(N) units in January 1964, 3056/65/68 were reclassified as 4 GRI units from 4th January 1964 and renumbered 3086/87/88 respectively. They remained at work on the Portsmouth Direct route alongside 4-BUF units, although they did work occasionally on the Central section. All three units were later repainted into all-blue livery with full yellow ends (3086 in Sep-69, 3087 in Apr-67 and 3088 in Feb-69) the griddle cars then being lettered 'Griddle' at the buffet end and 'Buffet' at the bar end of the coach.

These units outlasted the 4-BUFs in traffic and were (along with non-standard cafeteria car unit 3072) the last remaining 'Portsmouth' stock with catering facilities.

These four units were transferred to the Central section from 1st November 1970 and were last used on 30th April 1971, units 3086 and 3087 having been used on a farewell tour on 8th February 1971. All three units were moved from Lovers Walk to Ford on 1st May 1971 for storage before moving on to Gatwick (8th May 1971) being stored there out of use until official withdrawal of all three units on 20th November 1971. All three were then hauled to Selhurst for stripping c.27th November 1971.

Formation of 4-GRI Units 3086 to 3088

Unit no. Diag no.	MBS 2114	TGS 2572	TFK 2505	MBS 2114	Withdrawn	Sent for scrapping	Notes
Code	A-1A	BC-2B	BD	A			Codes from c.1963
3086	11143 (3056)	12605 (3065)	12245 (3056)	11144 (3056)	20-Nov-71	9-Jun-72	
3087	11202 (3065)	12602 (3068)	12237 (3065)	11162 (3065)	20-Nov-71	20-Jan-73*	* Date taken into departmental stock as unit 054.
3088	11167 (3068)	12609 (3056)	12240 (3068)	11168 (3068)	20-Nov-71	9-Jun-72	
Departmental unit 054							
ADB975255	23-Nov-74	6-Jun-75	Former unit 3087				

Bulleid's first design was the interior arrangement of the Buffet cars for the Mid-Sussex Line's 4-BUF sets. The art-deco styling was brash and contemporary. These were the first coaches to have his light green exterior livery and they certainly brought much-needed improvement on these services.

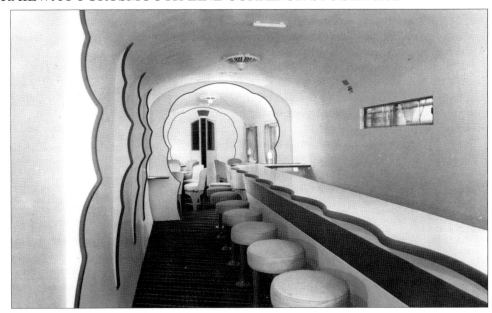

Individual Unit Notes 3086 - 3088	
3086	TFK 12245 sent from Selhurst to Hoo Junction c.Dec-71 where body broken-up and underframe returned to Stewarts Lane for conversion, being used as basis for long-welded-rail carrying wagon DB975528. MBSs 11143 and 11144 and TGS 12605 all hauled from Selhurst to Shalford 13-Jan-72 for storage, moving to Salisbury 1-Jun-72 and forward for scrapping to T. W. Ward Ltd, Briton Ferry 9-Jun-72 (although still in Margam Yard later that month).
3087	Unit ran under own power from Selhurst to Eastleigh 5-Feb-72 and then used for pressure heating /ventilation tests in the buffet car in connection with the new PEP stock. Unit taken into departmental stock 20-Jan-73. Unit stored at Micheldever after withdrawal and moved to T W Ward Ltd, Beighton 6-Jun-75 for scrapping.
3088	Unit hauled from Selhurst to Shalford 13-Jan-72 for storage, moving to Salisbury 1-Jun-72 and forward for scrapping to T. W. Ward Ltd, Briton Ferry 9-Jun-72 (although still in Margam Yard later that month).

4-PUL Units 3054 to 3059 & 4-COR(N) Units 3065 to 3071

A major stock reshuffle took place in January 1964 between Friday 3rd and Monday 6th. This involved downgrading many services with advertised catering facilities to Buffet or Minibuffet status, removing all the restaurant facilities. It brought spare 4-CEP and 4-BEP units from the South Eastern Division's 'Boat Train Pool' into regular service on the Victoria to Portsmouth /Bognor route, displacing a number of 4-COR and nine 4-BUF units which were moved to the South Western Division to work on the Waterloo to Portsmouth line.

This left the twelve then remaining 4-RES units without employment as they were displaced by 4-BUF units on the Portsmouth Direct route. These units were briefly stored before being taken to Lovers Walk for reforming over four weekends. The trailer restaurant seconds were withdrawn (officially from 25th January 1964) and the units were all reformed with trailers from disbanded 6-PUL and 6-PAN units, five 6-PUL and three 6-PAN units coming out of service as the last phase of the stock reshuffle.

These 6-PUL and 6-PAN units being the units with motor coaches in the worst condition with some equipment from them being removed for inclusion in the new 4-CIG and 4-BIG units being constructed at York.

The 4-RES units involved were 3054/55/57/59/61/62/64/66/67/69/70/71 and the first five became 4 PUL units 3054 - 3057/59 with unit 3061 being renumbered as 3056. The remaining seven became 4-COR (N) units 3065 – 3071 with unit 3062 being renumbered as 3065 and unit 3064 becoming 3068.

The reason for the '(N)' suffix on the 4-COR (N) is understood to have been provided in order to emphasise the units' lack of catering facilities; up to that point all units with numbers beginning 30xx had some form of catering.

The 4 PUL units included a former 6-PUL composite Pullman car which seated 12 first and 16 second; these weighed 43 tons. The former dining area in the 4-RES TFK was now regarded as ordinary first class seating and this coach therefore seated 42 first so that the overall unit seating capacity was now 42 first and 104 second plus 12 first and 16 second in the Pullman car. The overall weight was now 169 tons and each unit was 267' 0" long.

In the 4-COR(N) units the TRS was replaced by a former 6-PAN TSK which seated 68 second and weighed 31½ tons. The former dining area was again now regarded as ordinary first class seating so the overall unit capacity was 42 first and 172 second. Overall unit length was unchanged at 264' 6" but the weight was reduced to 157½ tons.

These units were used on the Central Division, mainly on Victoria to Littlehampton services through 1964 and into 1965 and enabled (for the first time) formation of twelve coach trains with all coaches having access to the Pullman car.

When these units were again displaced by new 4-CIG and 4-BIG stock all were reformed again into standard 4-COR formation using 6-PUL and 6-PAN trailers. Reclassified as 4-COR they became unit numbers 3159 - 3168.

However, in October 1964 two units each had one MBS removed (to be used in 'Push-Pull' tests) and were replaced by MBSs from standard 4-COR units. As a consequence units 3056 and 3059 were disbanded with the two 4-COR MBSs returning to their original units and the remaining two ex 4-RES MBSs being used together to form part of 'new' unit 3160.

Unit 3070 was also disbanded so that only ten 'new' 4-COR units were formed from the twelve 4-PUL and 4-COR(N) units.

Most units were out of use by early 1966 and units 3065/7 were sent to Eastleigh for reforming in February whilst units 3055/7/66 were stored at Ford for a while before going to Eastleigh in late March 1966.

Units 3054/69/71 were retained serviceable as a spare train (used 24th March 1966) until they also went to Eastleigh in June 1966.

Formation of 4-PUL Units 3054 to 3059

Unit no. Diag no.	Date	MBS 2114	TCP (Sch. No.)	TFK 2505	MBS 2114	Disbanded	New No.	Notes
Code		A-1A	?	BD	A			Codes from c.1963
3054	Jan-64	11177	Clara (3020)	12248	11140	Jun-66	3161	Clara - Pullman schedule no.269
3055	Jan-64	11142	Gwladys (3017)	12246	11141	Mar-66	3162	Gwladys - Pullman schedule no.272
3056	Jan-64	11153 (3061)	Ethel (3018)	12233 (3061)	11154 (3061) 11214	Jun-65	3160	Ethel - Pullman schedule no.270
3057	Feb-64	11145	Elinor (3004) Lorna (3008)	12247 12276 [9] (3037)	11146	Mar-66	3163	[9] Former 6-PAN TFK Diagram 2506. Elinor - Pullman schedule no.295 Lorna - Pullman schedule no.277
3059	Feb-64	11149	Enid (3014) Alice (3009)	12242	11172 11128	Jun-65	3160	Enid Pullman schedule no.296 Alice Pullman schedule no.271

Formation of 4 COR(N) Units 3065 to 3071

Unit no. Diag no.	Date	MBS 2114	TSK 2010	TFK 2505	MBS 2114	Disbanded	New No.	Notes
Code		A-1A	BB	BD	A			Codes from c.1963
3065	Mar-64	11155 (3062)	10034 (3027)	12235 (3062)	11156 (3062)	Feb-66	3164	
3066	Jan-64	11163	10033 (3027)	12238	11164	Mar-66	3165	

3067	Jan-64	11165	10046 (3033)	12239	11166	Feb-66	3166	
3068	19-Jan-64	11159 (3064)	10045 (3033)	12236 (3064)	11160 (3064)	24-Aug-65	3159	
3069	Jan-64	11169	10042 (3031)	12241	11170	Jun-66	3167	
3070	Feb-64	11171	10041 (3031)	12250	11229	c.May-65	601	
3071	Feb-64	11173	10044 (3014)	12243	12274	Jun-66	3168	

Individual Unit Notes 3054 - 3059

3054	Unit disbanded Jun-66 and Pullman Car Clara withdrawn 2-Jul-66, TFK 12248 to loose stock. Replaced by TSK 10003 (ex 6-PUL 3003) and TCK 11765 (ex 6 PUL 3005) and unit reclassified as 4 COR numbered 3161. Both *Clara* and 12248 stored at Hove by Aug-66, *Clara* being moved to A. King, Wymondham for scrapping 24-Sep-66. TFK 12248 at Selhurst by Jul-67, condemned 21-Oct-67 and scrapped by Armytage, Sheepbridge arriving 27-Apr-68, moving from Hove. Coach cut-up 7-May-68.
3055	Unit disbanded Mar-66 at Lovers Walk and both trailers moved to Hove 21-Mar-66. Pullman Car Gwladys withdrawn 26-Mar-66 and moved to A. King Ltd, Wymondham 24-Sep-66 for scrapping. TFK 12246 to loose stock until condemned 21-Oct-67 and scrapped by Armytage, Sheepbridge arriving 4-May-68, moving from Andover. Coach cut-up 25-May-68. Replaced by TSK 10053 (ex 6-PAN 3037) and TCK 11755 (ex 6-PUL 3003) with unit reclassified as 4-COR 3162.
3056	Unit formed Jan-64 with 4 RES vehicles (renumbered from unit 3061) and 6 PUL Pullman Car Ethel (ex 3018). MBS 11154 to Push-Pull tests from Jul-64, later to 6 TC 601 from May-65 and replaced by 11214 (ex 3148). Unit disbanded Jun-65 and 11214 returned to 3148. MBS 11153 to 4 COR 3160 from Aug-65. Pullman Car Ethel and TFK 12233 both moved to Hassocks for storage 24-Jul-65. Ethel withdrawn 30-Oct-65 and moved for scrapping 4-Jun-66 from there to A. King, Wymondham. TFK 12233 to loose stock and stored until condemned 21-Oct-67 and moved from Hassocks for scrapping to Armytage, Sheepbridge arriving 6-Apr-68; cut-up 12-Apr-68.
3057	Unit reformed Feb-66 with Pullman Car *Elinor* withdrawn 12-Feb-66 and TFK 12247 to loose stock, both moved to Hove for storage 21-Mar-66. Replaced by Pullman Car *Lorna* (ex 6 PUL 3008) and TFK 12276 (ex 6 PAN 3037). This coach had all first class seating in compartments, weighed 31 tons and was 59' 0" long, giving unit a non-standard length of 262' 8" and weight of 168 tons. *Elinor* moved to Chichester 26-May-66 and on for scrapping to Bird Group, Bynea 1-Jun-66, whilst 12247 moved to Selhurst by Jul-67 and condemned 21-Oct-67. Unit disbanded Mar-66 with Pullman Car *Lorna* withdrawn 26-Mar-66 and scrapped by A. King Ltd, Wymondham c.Oct-66. TFK 12276 stored as loose stock until withdrawn 21-Oct-67 being scrapped (along with 12247 above) at Armytage, Sheepbridge; 12247 moving from Hove arriving 27-Apr-68 /cut-up 14-May-68 and 12276 moving from Andover arriving 4-May-68 /cut-up 11-May-68. Replaced by TSK 10054 (ex 6-PAN 3037) and TCK 11788 (ex 6-PUL 3008) with unit reclassified as 4-COR and renumbered 3163.
3059	Unit formed Jan-64 with Pullman Car *Enid* (ex 6 PUL 3014). MBS 11172 to Push-Pull tests from Jul-64 and replaced by 11128 (ex 3124). Pullman Car *Enid* withdrawn Oct-64 and moved to Micheldever for storage, (*scrapped c.Oct-65, location unknown*) and replaced by Pullman Car *Alice* (ex 3009). Unit disbanded Jun-65 and MBS 11128 returned to 3124. MBS 11149 to 'new' 4-COR 3160 Aug-65. Pullman Car *Alice* to 6-PUL 3041 Nov-65. TFK 12242 stored at Hassocks from 24-Jul-65 as loose stock until condemned 21-Oct-67; moved for scrapping to Armytage, Sheepbridge arriving 6-Apr-68 and cut-up 12-Apr-68.

Individual Unit Notes 3065 - 3071

3065	Unit formed Mar-64 with 4-RES vehicles (renumbered ex unit 3062) and TSK 10034 (ex 6-PAN 3027). Unit disbanded Feb-66 and TFK 12235 stored as loose stock, moving to Selhurst by Jul-67 until condemned 21-Oct-67 and sent to Ashford where body broken-up and underframe used for Crane Runner DS70281. Replaced by 6-PUL TCK 11787 (ex 3008) and unit reclassified as 4-COR 3164.

3066	Unit disbanded Mar-66 and TFK 12238 stored as loose stock, moving to Selhurst by Jul-67 until condemned 21-Oct-67 and scrapped at Armytage, Sheepbridge (arriving 27-Apr-68) moving from Hove. Coach cut-up 9-May-68. Replaced by 6-PUL TCK 11752 (ex 3013) and unit reclassified as 4-COR 3165.
3067	Unit disbanded Feb-66 and TFK 12239 stored as loose stock, moving to Selhurst by Jul-67 until condemned 21-Oct-67 and scrapped at Armytage, Sheepbridge (arriving 27-Apr-68) moving from Hove. Coach cut-up 8-May-68. Replaced by 6 PUL TCK 11751 (ex 3013) and unit reclassified as 4-COR 3166.
3068	Unit formed 27-Jan-64 with 4-RES vehicles (renumbered ex 3064) and TSK 10045 (ex 6 PAN 3033). Unit disbanded 24-Aug-65 at Lancing and TFK 12236 stored as loose stock at Micheldever until condemned 21-Oct-67 and scrapped at Armytage, Sheepbridge, moving 10-Apr-68 (arriving 28-May-68 /cut-up 12-Jun-68). Replaced by 6-PUL TCK 11773 (ex 3018) and unit reclassified as 4-COR 3159.
3069	Unit disbanded Jun-66 and TFK 12241 stored as loose stock, initially at Hove and moved to Selhurst by Jul-67 until condemned 21-Oct-67 and scrapped at Armytage, Sheepbridge (arriving 27-May-68) moving from Hove. Coach cut-up 7-Jun-68. Replaced by 6-PUL TCK 11784 (ex 3001) and unit reclassified as 4-COR 3167.
3070	Unit disbanded c.May-65 and MBS 11229 and TSK 10041 both to 6 TC 601. TFK 12250 stored as loose stock at Micheldever until condemned 21-Oct-67 and scrapped at Armytage, Sheepbridge (moving 10-Apr-68 /arriving 27-May-68 /cut-up 6-Jun-68). MBS 11171 to 3147 from Jan-67.
3071	Unit disbanded Jun-66. TFK 12243 stored as loose stock until condemned 21-Oct-67 and scrapped at Armytage, Sheepbridge (arriving 27-Apr-68) moving from Hove. Coach cut-up 3-May-68. Replaced by 6 PUL TCK 11776 (ex 3007) and unit reclassified as 4-COR 3168.

Life start and life end.
Above - *manufacturer's view of MBS 11159 from Unit No 3064.*

Left - *Brighton Top yard on 30 November 1977. Former 4-COR MBS from set No 3131 stands attached to a Mid-Sussex line buffet car whilst immediately alongside is 5 BEL unit No 3053. (See disposal detail on p 19.)*
C Burnham

and speaking of EMU's....

The Story of EMU Names

Alan Postlethwaite

I was intrigued by the article in SW27 on the 2-BIL units. The origin of this acronym, however, like that of other SR electric units, is a myth. The true story is that they were all named by Ernie Blagott, in charge of the little-known Naming Department (Locomotives, Trains and Stations) based at Waterloo station. The electric names are abbreviations of words relating to his life. Ernie joined the L&SWR in 1920 after leaving the Army as a subaltern. So his first act was to call all the SR electric units 3-SUB or 4-SUB according to rank. When new variations arrived, he called one of them Lavender Hill where he lived (4-LAV) and the rest after his snooker mates at the Union Jack Club, namely Noel (2-NOL), Harry (2-HAL) and Bill (2-BIL). To keep his bosses happy, he spread a rumour that these names were somehow related to lavatory arrangements - his Water-loos as he liked to call them.

During his salad days, Ernie proposed to his future wife Isabelle (5-BEL) in Kensington Gardens by Peter Pan's statue (6-PAN) while wearing a rather fetching Fair Isle pullover (6-PUL). They took their honeymoon in Cornwall (4-COR) at Restormel (4-RES) where they watched a Buffalo Bill film (4-BUF) on their wedding night. When Ernest Percival Blagott retired in the early 1950s, his final act was to name the latest units after himself (4-EPB). And in memory of his brother who died in Australia, he called the whole lot EMUs. A job well done, I think.

One of Ernie's other duties was to think up names to confuse aliens. In this photo at Dorking North, both units are classified as 4-SUB but one is ex-LB&SCR wooden steam stock while the other is all-steel to the design of Mr Bulleid. Another trick was to give trains on the same service different headcodes. In this example, both '17' and 'I' mean Waterloo to Horsham. His special skills extended to station names. That is why North Dulwich is almost due south of East Dulwich and due north of West Dulwich. Furthermore, Canterbury East is west of South Canterbury and due south of Canterbury West. Another feather in Ernie's cap, I think. May his legacy endure!

Ernie disliked being photographed. He had a squarish face and wore a monocle, looking rather like the RH train.
He is of course fictitious and any resemblance to a real person, past or present, is unintentional and coincidental. (But then this is the April issue.......Ed.)

Rail Tour Heaven

Andrew Harris

The 1950s saw the start of Rail Tours, usually organised by long established railway societies with the willing participation of railway officials of all grades. It was a good opportunity to travel on the lines, some closed to passengers for up to twenty years and others about to be closed or behind unusual or historic locomotives. The Southern Region was not forgotten and I was fortunate to be able to participate in many trips having returned south in the summer of 1951 after over five years in Glasgow.

The first was organised by the Stephenson Locomotive Society on the 6 October 1951 starting at Kensington Olympia at 14.30. This had only a partial Southern involvement over long electrified lines which would rarely see a steam hauled passenger train. Hauled in its entirety by LNER B1 4-6-0 No. 61175 it mainly covered lines in the NE and NW of the capital reaching Southern metals at Richmond and travelling via Twickenham and the Hounslow loop to Clapham Junction before returning to Olympia due 17.32.

My next on the 29 March 1952, was the first of many run by the Railway Correspondence and Travel Society. Named the 'North East London Rail Tour', its 45½ mile route had less than five miles over the Southern but was so popular that two trains of eight main-line coaches had to be provided for the over 700 participants, the trains running 30 minutes apart. Starting from London Bridge the first working at 14.20 had ex GER. J69 0-6-0T haulage whilst the second, on which I was a passenger, left 12 minutes later for the run to New Cross Gate behind E1 4-4-0 No 31507. Due to unseasonal blizzard conditions, snow and ice caused major problems especially at Cheshunt where the locomotives had not only to run round but take on water. Consequently the schedule disintegrated but we could take

heart that as it was also the day of the university Boat Race, no doubt the rowers suffered more than us. Southern metals were regained via the Metropolitan widened lines through Farringdon with the train terminating at Cannon Street. Thus a normal five- minute journey between two adjacent stations but scheduled to take 3 hours 45 minutes on its roundabout journey was eventually exceeded by 1 hour 37 minutes.

Less than a month later on the 18 May 1952 it was the turn of the RCTS Isle of Wight Tour (13/-). In complete contrast, this was a day of sunny weather with travel from Portsmouth on the M.V.Brading whilst at Ryde Pier Head a two coach train was waiting, headed by E1 0-6-0T No. W3 'Ryde', for our party of 124. Departing at 11.22 a non-stop run was made to Newport where nearly an hour allowed a visit to the loco shed. After a further coach was added a return trip was made to Cowes. Back again at Newport, 02 0 -4-4T No W32 'Bonchurch' took over for a run to Freshwater stopping in each direction at Ningwood for an ordinary passenger train to pass. On leaving Newport for the third time the route was now via Merstone and the terminus at Ventnor West. Ours was believed to be the first Sunday

'Ryde' not at Ryde' but a Newport.

Tour engine and withdrawn but clean I3 No 32091.

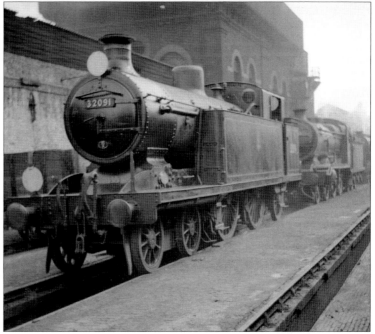

train since 1939 so the residents were surprised by its appearance. A return to Merstone, saw us reverse and take the line to Sandown where a further reversal occurred. Now it was north to Brading where everyone detrained and joined the Bembridge branch train headed by O2 0-4-4T No W14 'Fishbourne'. The final leg was behind 'Bonchurch' to Ryde St Johns where an hour was spent visiting the shed and works. Finally it was on to the Pier Head and eventual return to Portsmouth aboard the M.V. Southsea. This trip of nearly 77 miles did not quite cover the complete island although many years later I returned and took the electric train from Ryde through Sandown and on to Shanklin. By then of course the extension to Ventnor had long been closed.

The 5 October 1952 saw the running of the RCTS's *'Brighton Works Centenary Special'*, a truly ambitious undertaking comprising a steam-hauled all-Pullman train booked in the 60 minute non-stop schedule between London and the south coast town. Brighton Atlantic H2 4-4-2 No 32424 'Beachy Head' was in charge with eight Pullman cars, tare weight 319 tons, gross weight 340 tons, with approximately 284 passengers. We departed from Victoria at 10.14 and were banked as far as Ebury Bridge by 2P 2-6-2T No 41296. Speed was up to 61 mph at Streatham Common but negated by signals at South Croydon, bringing matters down to 17 mph. After this it was full regulator again with 71½ mph at Earlswood, 74

BRITISH RAILWAYS (S)
This ticket is issued subject to the Bye-laws, Regulations and Conditions contained in the Publications and Notices of and applicable to the Railway Executive.
The Railway Correspondence & Travel Society
Bisley Tramway & North West Surrey Rail Tour
Available on DAY of issue ONLY.
Waterloo to BROOKWOOD
Returning to VICTORIA
including trip over the
BISLEY BRANCH
THIRD CLASS 23rd. November 1952
NOT TRANSFERABLE.
0190

BRITISH RAILWAYS (S)
This ticket is issued subject to the Bye-laws, Regulations and Conditions contained in the Publications and Notices of and applicable to the Railway Executive.
The Railway Correspondence & Travel Society
Available on Day of issue ONLY
Eastleigh to
SOUTHAMPTON CTL.
and Tour of Fawley Branch and Southampton Docks
THIRD CLASS 17th MAY 1953
NOT TRANSFERABLE
0046

Top left - No 30757 'Earl of Mount Edgecombe' ready to depart what was then Platform 4 at Eastleigh for Fawley.

Bottom left - V2 No 60908 standing-in for a Bulleid Pacific and seen passing the approach/exit to Eastleigh shed.

Opposite top - D15 No 30464 at Waterloo ready to depart for Salisbury, 28 June 1953.

mph at Balcombe and 75 mph at Haywards Heath, thus Brighton was reached in 58 minutes 40 seconds (54 min 45 sec net). Inside the works it was good to see new steam locomotives actually being built, Standard CL4 2-6-4T's Nos 80048 & 49 almost complete with the frames for the next two ready. Under repair were C 0-6-0 Nos. 31102, 31227, 31579, H 0-4-4T No. 31158, K 2-6-0 No. 32344, E6 0-6-2T No. 32409, E3 0-6-2T No. 32462, E4 0-6-2T No. 32507, C2X 0-6-0 No. 32548, 4P 2-6-4T Nos. 42066, 42101, Main Line Diesel Electric No. 10202, and Diesel Shunters Nos. 15216, 15230. *Beachy Head* was moved on to one of the works roads and the works shunter No 377S A1X 0-6-0 T (32635) was also on show. At the locomotive shed the three engines which had all carried the name *Brighton*, A1X 0-6-0T No. 32640, E5 0-6-2T No. 32587

and V 4-4-0 No. 30915 together with the last withdrawn I3 4-4-2T No. 32091 were specially lined up for photos. Also on shed were S15 4-6-0 No. 30833, V 4-4-0 No. 30906 *Sherborne*, P 0-6-0T Nos. 31027, 31325, 31558, E3 0-6-2T Nos. 32166/68-70, K 2-6-0 Nos. 32337-39/42/45/53, D3 0-4-4T Nos. 32365/68/72/76, H2 4-4-2 Nos. 32421 South Foreland, 32422 *North Foreland* C2X 0-6-0 Nos. 32434/37/38/40/42, E4 0-6-2T Nos. 32482/85/92, 32513-15/18/66, E5 0-6-2T Nos. 32573/83/86/88, WC 4-6-2 Nos. 34045 *Ottery St Mary* 34046 *Braunton*, 34047 *Callington* 2P 2-6-2T No. 41299, 4P 2-6-4T Nos. 42070/87, 42103/05/06 and Std. 4 2-6-4T Nos. 80016/31-33/46. A further treat was in store in that A1X 0-6-0T No. 32636 *(Fenchurch)* operating a two coach push-pull set, made several return trips from Brighton to Kemp Town. The return from Brighton at 16.28 was equally enjoyable with 72 mph from Hassocks to Keymer Junction, 71½ mph at Three Bridges and 79½ mph at Horley resulting in an arrival at Victoria 14 seconds over the hour due to more signal checks (54 min 30 sec net). On the journey, coffee was served on the way down and afternoon tea on the return. All in all an excellent organised trip with much credit due to those involved. Such was its success that it was repeated on the 19 October, although this time bad weather somewhat spoiled the day. As an aside I only travelled once on the electric "Belle" on the 29 July 1951 from East Croydon to London Bridge!

The Bisley Tramway had closed on the 19 July 1952 and as the track was about to be lifted the RCTS quickly arranged an afternoon special. 'The Bisley Tramway and North West Surrey Rail Tour' ran on the 23 November 1952 starting from Waterloo at 12.38. The seven-coach train was hauled by 0395 0-6-0 No 30577 which took the East Putney line to Wimbledon and down the main line to Brookwood, arrival at 13.38, with a maximum speed of 48 mph near Weybridge. M7 0-4-4T No 30027 made two return trips to Bisley Camp to enable the 300 participants to make the journey. I remember that on my return trip I joined at least eight others on the footplate for the three minute journey. The main train again with No 30577 left at 14.45 and at Sturt Lane Jc the Ascot line was taken with 60 mph attained for ½ mile through Bagshot and 58 mph after Virginia Water. Not bad going for a 45 year-old goods' engine! After Clapham Junction the route via Longhedge Jc and Stewarts Lane was taken into Victoria with a five minute early arrival at 16.00. Not appreciated at the time was that No. 30577's driver was none other than A.E. (Bert) Hooker of 'Merchant Navy' fame. (For a photograph of 30577 at Brookwood on this tour see S.W. No19 page 19.)

The next Southern trip on the 17 May 1953, was notable not only for the motive power used and route taken but for the repercussions of an event which had occurred on the 24 April at Axminster. On the latter date the driving axle of MN 4-6-2 No. 35020 *Bibby Line* had fractured at speed and as a result the complete class of 30 locomotives had been withdrawn from traffic on the 12 May. This then was the setting for what was provided for the 'Southampton Docks and Fawley Branch Rail Tour'. London members travelled behind WC 4-6-2 No. 34010 *Sidmouth* which was banked out of Waterloo by LNER V2 No. 60908, seen later passing Eastleigh on a Bournemouth train. On arrival at Eastleigh, the works were visited first and where, due to the repercussions mentioned, there were no fewer than 12 members of the 'Merchant Navy' class present with another seen later at the shed. The works and shed also had a veritable plethora of machines, M7, T9, 700, S15, Q, N15, LN, V, E1, E4, WC/BB, MN, 4P 2-6-4T and the frames of USA 0-6-0T 1261 On shed there was similar variety M7,

USA, B4, 02, T9, 700, D15, H15, S15, Q, 0395, C14, N15, PDSW 0-6-2T, LN, V, Z, U, L1, E1, E6, E4, Q1, WC, MN, 2P 2-6-2T, 4P 2-6-4T, Std 4 2-6-0, Std 3 2-6-2T and three diesel shunters. To haul our train of five coaches and a van from Eastleigh station No 30757 *Earl of Mount Edgcumbe* had been specially brought up from Plymouth and having been extremely well cleaned made a bright sight in the sunshine. There was an 11 minute late departure at 15.21, due to extra coaches being needed, followed by a straightforward run to Fawley, including a 5½ minute stop at Southampton Central. At the end of the Southern metals the Esso Petroleum GEC 0-4-4-0 Diesel was on view. For the return journey, which departed 7½ minutes late at 16.22½, behind USA 0-6-0T No 30062 the route was through Central Station again and round the west chord of Northam curve to the Ocean Terminal where an 80 minute stop allowed for the shed and other parts of the docks to be viewed. Not surprisingly Southampton Docks shed was seen with a number of USA 0-6-0Ts present. Leaving at 18.16 a visit was made to Berth 50 which had been built as a marine terminal for the BOAC flying boat services. The train's arrival caused considerable surprise to the various anglers who were using the quay. We then ran along local roads through the Town Quay, New Docks and Millbrook, terminating at Central Station one minute early at 19.09. Return to London was behind BB 4-6-2 34065 *Hurricane*.

Just over one month later on the 28 June 1953 the RCTS ran its longest rail tour at 380½ miles. 'The 25th Anniversary Special' (£1.6s.6d), was scheduled to make fast runs from London to Exeter and return. The seven coach train was headed by D15 4-4-0 No 30464, driver A.E. Hooker, again, was due to depart Waterloo at 9.45 but because of the late arrival of the stock was away 8½ minutes late from the Windsor line platforms. Notwithstanding two PWS. on the journey to Salisbury, that at Fleet bringing speed down to 12 mph, the journey was achieved in 4½ minutes over the 91 minute schedule. (90

BRITISH RAILWAYS (S)
This ticket is issued subject to the Bye-laws,
Regulations and Conditions contained in the
Publications and Notices of and applicable to the
Railway Executive.
The Railway Correspondence & Travel Society
971   25th. Anniversary Special   971
Available on DAY of issue ONLY
WATERLOO to EXETER
Including trip on
LYME REGIS Branch Returning
EXETER to PADDINGTON
THIRD CLASS   28th. J U N E 1953
NOT TRANSFERABLE

0058   0058

BRITISH RAILWAYS (S)
This ticket is issued subject to the Bye-laws,
Regulations and Conditions contained in the
Publications and Notices of and applicable to the
Railway Executive.
Railway Correspondence & Travel Society.
EAST SUSSEX RAIL TOUR
THREE BRIDGES AND RETURN
Via EAST GRINSTEAD(H.L.),HEATHFIELD
POLEGATE,LEWES,HORSTED KEYNES and
EAST GRINSTEAD (L.L.) and (H.L.)
BY SPECIAL TRAIN
THIRD CLASS.   4th, OCT, 1953
NOT TRANSFERABLE

0092   0092

The last survivor of the South Eastern 'E' class, No. 31166 at Ashford ready to double-head the special back to London. 12 September 1954.

min net). At Salisbury the D15 was replaced by T9 4-4-0 No. 30711 which left 13½ minutes late but took 67 min 40 sec (64 min net) as against a schedule of 72 minutes to the stop at Axminster, 78½ mph was achieved at Gillingham, 83½ at Millbourne Port and 86 mph at Sherborne. A stop of nearly three hours was arranged at Axminster to enable two trips to take place on the Lyme Regis branch which was about to celebrate its 50th anniversary since opening. The branch engine was 0415 4-4-2T No 30583 which I had seen on the East Kent Light Railway in April 1945 and had been repurchased by the Southern in 1946. This was piloted by A1X 0-6-0T No. 32662. Sister engine No 32646 (LSWR 734) which had been present on the opening day, had been requested for us but this had failed to make the journey westward. Among those welcoming us at Lyme was 80 year -old Mr G.F Hawker who had been on the footplate on the opening day. Back to Axminster and another fast run took place with a maximum of 83 mph at Whimple. Signals, however, delaying the arrival at Exeter Central which was reached in 38 min 20 sec (35 min 30 sec net), schedule 37 minutes. After a short stop the train descended to St David's where Star 4-6-0 No. 4056 *Princess Margaret* had been planned to make a fast non-stop return via Westbury. Unfortunately due to engineering works the special had to be diverted via Bristol with a five minute stop at Temple Meads resulting in a 4 hr, 25 min schedule. However, the less said the better about that particular trip as it slowly descended from bad to worse eventually taking over 4¾ hours from Exeter to Paddington.

Two more Rail Tours completed the year, the first on the 4 October 1953 with a delightful wander round "East Sussex" for 12/-. Starting from Three Bridges at 13.00 behind the last surviving D3 0-4-4T No 32390, we had the

same two-coach push-pull set used on the Kemp Town specials the previous year. However on this occasion normal working was adopted with the loco running round when required as the set had arrived the wrong way round. The tour took in East Grinstead High Level to Eridge and down the Cuckoo Line to Polegate where the first reversal took place. Then along the main line to Lewes East Jc. and under special arrangements via the goods line (which was part of the original route) and into the tunnel at the north end of the station. Then back into the station where the engine ran round. After a short stop, the Bluebell line was taken with a stop for water at Sheffield Park. At East Grinstead Low Level the goods spur was traversed to reach the High Level platforms and back to Three Bridges, due 17.18.

Six days later on the 10 October 1953 another RCTS trip, the 'London Area Rail Tour' had a minor Southern input. This covered all four B.R. regions serving London and was handled with two trains headed by LNER N1 0-6-2Ts. The start was from Marylebone at 14.05, the Southern Region reached after passing Kensington Olympia. Then it was into Battersea Yard for water and through Loughborough Junction to Farringdon, where everyone alighted to join a non-corridor set for the run to Kentish Town to join another train. Of general interest not only was there a non-stop run around the Wembley Stadium loop but from Bromley the North London line was taken via Bow and the East to South curve at Dalston Junction to terminate at Broad Street at 18.35.

The first tour of 1954 to have a Southern influence was perhaps surprisingly, called 'The Swindon and Highworth Special' (£1,3s.), on 25 April but which started and finished on Southern metals. The title is of course self-explanatory but the sight of the two GWR 9000 Class 4-4-0s at the head of an eight coach train at Platform 7 at Victoria was surreal. In fact this was probably the first (G) WR destined departure from Victoria since Ealing and Southall services were discontinued in 1915! The train was

10 October 1954, T9 No. 30729 at Cheddington and Bletchley.

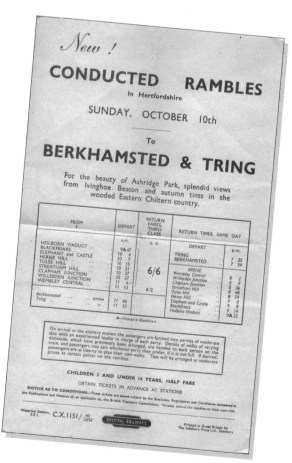

hauled by No. 9023 piloting No. 9021 and although due away at 10.12, departure was not until 10.35 travelling via Stewarts Lane to Kensington Olympia. The return journey followed the outward one as far as Reading and down the war-time connection to Reading New Jc. Here the train engine, GWR 2-8-0 No. 4707, was uncoupled and replaced by H16 4-6-2T No. 30517 which ran via Ascot, Virginia Water west curve to Chertsey for a water stop, Weybridge, Wimbledon and East Putney to Clapham Junction. A maximum speed of 55 mph was reached at Sunningdale and almost 50 mph at Raynes Park. At Clapham Junction No 30517 was replaced by C 0 -6-0 No. 31480 for the last stage via Stewarts Lane arriving at platform 2, Victoria at 20.24 (due 20.18).

Another major trip at 189½ miles took place on the 12 September 1954 almost in its entirety on Kentish lines. Named the 'Invicta Special' it did however start from Liverpool Street at 9.47. The seven coach train with two carrying roof boards 'Invicta Special -Liverpool Street-Sheerness-Ashford-Blackfriars' left behind LNER J69 0-6-0T No 68630 piloting J68 No 68639 and of course took the East London line and ran as far as Blackheath. Here D 4-4-0 No 31737 took charge as far as Rainham where it was replaced by R 0-4 -4T No 31671 for a direct run to Sheerness, reverse and back via the Sittingbourne East curve and on to Faversham. D1 4-4-0 No 31505 replaced No 31671 for a run to Canterbury West. The connecting spur between the LC&DR and SER had been built during the 1914/18 war, closed in 1920, re-opened in 1941, closed again when the war ended but re-opened during the severe floods affecting the

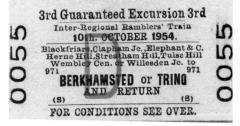

Top - The pairing of two E5s at Midhurst on the 'Hampshireman' special of 6 February 1955. The special is seen here at its photographic stop at Midhurst with the starting signal off for the Petersfield line.

Bottom - Late afternoon at West Meon. Some of the 540 passengers mingle with local residents to witness the very last passenger train ever to visit West Meon station. (Probably also the last train to make use of the water column.) Folklore has it that several travellers were reluctant to rejoin the train and despite much whistling by the crews it was only when the service actually started to move that the last scrambled aboard.

Kent coastline in February 1953. Our train was also probably the last one to travel between Canterbury Jc 'A' and 'B' signal boxes. Then on to Minster and down to Deal and on by the Kearsney loop to Kearsney station. At this point No. 31737 was waiting to take over the train again past Dover and Folkestone, noting No DS1169 a 4wDM acquired a few years earlier for civil engineering defences at the Warren. A nearly three-hour stop at Ashford allowed visits to the Works and shed. At the Works were examples of classes C, H, E, N, D, U, D1, L1, U1, W, K, E5X, E4, E5, and Q1, 0-6-0 No 33024. I regret I later mislaid the list I had made of engines seen at the nearby shed. For the return to London, the last surviving E 4-4-0 No. 31166 was provided as pilot for No 31737, good speeds were obtained with a maximum of 70 mph near Headcorn. At Tonbridge the Redhill line was taken but only as far as Edenbridge where the Crowhurst spur took us on to the Oxted line as far as Selsdon. Then the Mid-Kent line to Lewisham Jc, finally terminating at Blackfriars a few minutes before the scheduled time of 20.21. It should be noted that No. 31737 had run a creditable 121 miles on the tour.

The last trip of the year on the 10 October 1954 could be described as an add-on rail tour. In this period of the 50s a very popular series of excursions was run for the benefit of ramblers. Calling to pick-up at various suburban stations, the train would make several country stops from which organised walks of different lengths would either link you to one of the other stops or back to your starting point. On this occasion the train started from Blackfriars at 10.04 picking up at Elephant & Castle, Herne Hill, Tulse Hill and via the rarely-used curve to Leigham Jc and Streatham Hill to Clapham Junction. Then on to its last pick-ups at Willesden Junction and Wembley Central and setting-down at Berkhamstead and Tring. The RCTS took up 120 tickets and T9 4-4-0 No. 30729 was specially provided for the main line sections of the tour. The train of eight coaches had a further two added at Willesden Junction. For the record the Buckinghamshire Rail Tour (6s 6d Rambler portion, 10s 6d Rail Tour) included trips on the Aylesbury and Newport Pagnell branches and a visit to Wolverton Carriage Works. The main train was boarded at Bletchley for the return to Blackfriars due 21.14.

For the final journey to be described during this period and what was also to be a final Southern journey for a number of years, I was aboard 'The Hampshireman' (£1,

3s 6d) of 6 February 1955. This was planned to cover two lines which had both closed for passengers the day before and was also destined to be very popular, having no less than 540 passengers in ten coaches. Run on a bright and sunny day and departing from Waterloo at 9.15, the service started with Brighton Atlantic H2 4-4-2 No. 32421 *South Foreland*. The driver was once again Bert Hooker who was in fact an RCTS member. Routed via Barnes, Brentford, Whitton West Curve, Feltham, Staines, Chertsey, West Weybridge and Woking we arrived at Guildford where E5X 0-6-2Ts Nos. 32570/76 coupled bunker to bunker took over. The line through Cranleigh to Horsham was taken and after reversal down the Mid-Sussex to Pulborough we then took the officially closed line through Midhurst. At Petersfield the locos were uncoupled and replaced by a pair of T9s, Nos. 30301 and 30732 for the rest of the journey. Now it was down the Portsmouth Direct to Havant and thence west to Fareham. The Meon Valley line, which had also been closed officially from the previous day was gained through Funtley Tunnel and Knowle Junction with a photographic stop made at West Meon. Departing from here the route was on through Alton and Aldershot to Frimley, reverse, Farnborough, another reversal and then main line to Waterloo, due 17.07.

Traversing the route that was the home ground of the 4 COR sets and also that taken on
6 February 1955 by the 'Hampshireman' special, '700' 0-6-0 No 325 approached Buriton tunnel near Petersfield with the morning pick-up freight. The headcode is 'Nine Elms to Portsmouth via Woking and Guildford, 27 June 1950.

Philip M Alexander

(Seen right is an odd print taken by the photographer named. Does anyone know what happened to the SR collection of this man?)

The Ashford 1948 Wagon Photographs Notes by Mike King, Photographs BR Southern Region

While compiling the OPC series of Southern Wagon books, the authors made considerable use of a series of official photographs of newly-overhauled wagons, taken mostly during 1948, with a few into 1949. These were saved from Eastleigh Works by the late Ray Chorley and we christened them the Ashford 1948 wagon photographs – purely our own description – but a few were certainly taken at Eastleigh Carriage & Wagon Works during the period in question. The LSWR wagon pictures are characterised by being left-hand three-quarters views, while those taken of SECR, LBSCR and Southern subjects are normally right-hand three-quarters portraits. One wonders why the differentiation? The latter are mostly dated between April and June 1948, but some were later. The majority of the LSWR prints and just a few of the others have their background obliterated, although from time to time a print will surface with the background still visible, so probably more than one set of negatives were made.

What was most useful to us was their remarkable coverage of the wagon stock at that time and also that nearly all the wagons pictured had received a full overhaul and repaint – mostly in SR brown although there were a few in SR stone buff livery and others in the new British Railways white for refrigerated stock. One or two meat or insulated vans might also have been finished in passenger stock crimson lake or bauxite livery, but this is not entirely obvious from the pictures. All had an 'S' prefix to the running number in place of the previous company initials. At this time full repaints of wagons, particularly open wagons, were rare – patch or minimal repainting being very much the order of the day in those years of enforced austerity.

While the pictures speak for themselves, the reason why they were taken remains a mystery. Clearly they were taken to provide a snapshot of Southern wagon stock – the majority of extant diagrams being included in the 100+ pictures – but there must have been a purpose to the exercise. Not surprisingly, most SR standard designs were covered, as were almost 40 of LSWR origin, whereas only 15 ex-SECR wagons featured (mostly Maunsell/Lynes post-1915 designs) and, to date, just four ex-LBSCR wagon types have been found. Generally speaking, one wagon from each diagram was selected (but there were a few exceptions to this) so the person in charge must have been given clear directions as to what was required – and they must also have known their wagons! With but a few exceptions, Engineer's Department vehicles were excluded, so again, clear instructions were followed. Two of these exceptions were very ordinary 3-plank dropside ballast wagons – a type that might also be found amongst the traffic department wagons of the period. If other ED stock was photographed similarly, then these have yet to see the light of day. Only one departmental vehicle was included – this being an otherwise fairly normal LSWR covered goods van.

One is tempted to ask if similar pictures were taken by the other regions of British Railways – of course the Swindon publicity machine was well-oiled and habitually took photographs of ex-works goods vehicles, but what of the other regions and workshops? One possible use for these pictures would have been for the newly-formed British Railways Ideal Stocks Committee to ponder over while deliberating what form the nationalised wagon designs should take. If so, then it would be reasonable to expect similar sets of photographs to have been taken elsewhere – but why would there be a need to repaint and reletter the wagons to such a high standard? Workshops pride perhaps, but moreover, why bother to record wagons in excess of 40 years old and clearly long past their prime?

Of course, some diagrams failed to be represented and one must presume that no suitable examples presented themselves for overhaul during the period of the exercise. Or were some diagrams (e.g. several of LBSCR origin) deliberately ignored? A few are remarkable if only for their scarcity in 1948. Witness, for example, a Wainwright SECR outside-framed van and a LSWR batten truck – both types already down to single figure quantities by that time. For a good many of the wagons, this would prove to be their last overhaul before scrapping. Included here is a list of known subjects (not guaranteed to be 100% complete) as well as a small selection of pictures. Further selections will appear in future issues, as space permits.

Ex-LSWR stock			
SR Diagram	Number	Description	Remarks
1301B	s366	3-plank dropside	On timber u/frame
1301	S61799*	3-plank dropside	ED stock-on steel u/frame
1308A	s434	1-plank stone truck	On timber u/frame

1309	s7280	5-plank open goods	With round ends
1311	s4130	5-plank open goods	With square ends
1314	s7633	8-plank open goods	On timber u/frame
1314A	s7806	8-plank open goods	On steel u/frame
1316	s8477	8-plank open goods	18ft design
1316	s9111	8-plank open goods	15-ton example of last
1316	s9196	8-plank open goods	18ft design
1317	s61132	4 plank dropside stone wagon	SR built to LSWR design
1401	S42058	Ventilated fruit van	On timber u/frame
1402	s42139	Ventilated fruit van	On timber u/frame
1406	s42464	Covered goods wagon	High-roof type
1408	s44377	Covered goods wagon	On steel u/frame
1409	s42484	Covered goods wagon	On timber u/frame
1410	s44030	Covered goods wagon	Low-roof type, steel u/f
1410	s723s	Covered goods wagon	Departmental, timber u/f
1412	s44262	Covered goods wagon	Built for S&DJR in 1902
1461	s50089	Refrigerator van	White with black lettering
1462	s50175	Refrigerator van	White with black lettering
1463	s50461	Banana van	Stone with red lettering
1465	s50234	Insulated van	White with black lettering
1482	s51034	Ventilated meat van	Crimson lake livery?
1485	s51159	Ventilated meat van	Built for S&DJR in 1902
1502	s51745	Cattle wagon	High roof type
1541	s54830	10-ton goods brake van	With red ends & restricted use branding
1542	s56058	17-ton goods brake van	Prior to Isle of Wight transfer, ex no. 54948.
1543	s55022	24-ton goods brake van	May not have red ends
1544	s54961	20-ton goods brake van	With red ends
1545	s54958	20-ton goods brake van	May not have red ends
1547	s55095	25-ton goods brake van	With red ends
1595	s57566	Double bolster/batten wagon	
1597	s57839	Bogie bolster wagon	Coded bogie bolster C
1643	s60121	Road vehicle truck	Coded cartruck
1673	s61011	Machinery truck	Coded well A
1701	s61704	Gunpowder van	Coded cone
1732	S62948*	3-plank dropside	ED, ex-S&DJR in 1930

*These two are the only LSWR Engineer's vehicles to be included and so may be finished in red oxide livery, although this is not apparent from the pictures.

Total 38 vehicles. Some others extant in 1948 that were not included are opens to diagrams 1304/5/10/13, meat van 1481, cattle 1501/6, and "specials" 1671/76 – remarkably few considering that none of the wagons was exactly modern.

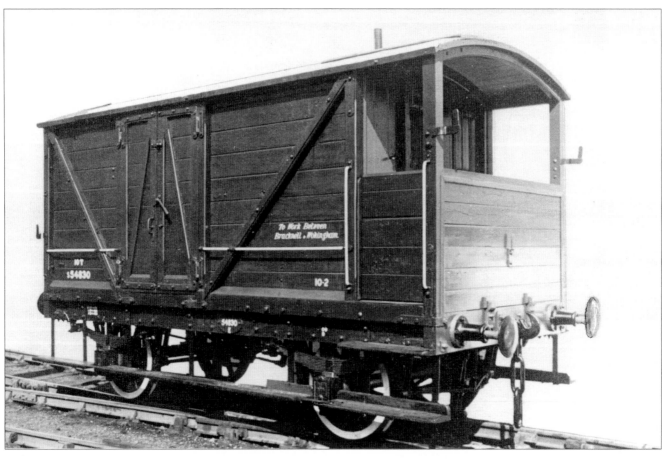

Opposite top - *Ex-LSWR 10-ton covered goods wagon s44030 – to Diagram 1410 and one of 254 still in ordinary traffic in 1948, although a considerable number could also be found amongst the departmental service stock. There were in excess of 1000 to this design in use at the Grouping, including vans on both timber and steel underframes and an equivalent timber-underframed wagon was photographed as s723s, later DS723 – the only departmental vehicle included in the series. No 44030 was completed in 1900 as LSWR no. 12312 and was then equipped with Panter's cross-lever brake gear. This may have satisfied the Board of Trade's subsequent requirement for either-side brake gear but it was less-than-robust in service and most wagons with it had more orthodox brake levers provided between 1918 and 1939. Although looking fairly presentable, the van had not been fully repainted and the former position of the initials 'SR' may just be seen on the sliding door, above the 10T marking. Note also odd wheelsets – those nearest are 10-spoke, farthest 8-spoke. The far buffer has also been replaced with one of ribbed pattern since original construction. Almost certainly its last overhaul, the wagon was withdrawn in 1953.*

Opposite bottom - *Ex-LSWR 10-ton brake van s54830, to Diagram 1541. Built in 1898 as LSWR no. 11091, so despite its immaculate appearance it was already 50 years old at the time! The red-painted ends show up well in this instance although not every brake van picture renders this feature so clearly. It seems remarkable that such an old van should be given such treatment so late in life, especially as it was not destined to travel far for the remainder of its existence. The restricted use board reads: "To work between Bracknell & Wokingham", from where the van was withdrawn in 1955. Diagram 1541 vehicles were selected by the Southern as their standard "light" (i.e. 10 tons tare or thereabouts) brake vans for branch line and local use from 1925 onwards and so were regularly stencilled for specific local workings – not always adhered to it must be said. In 1948 there were still in excess of 50 on the books (including about a dozen on the Isle of Wight) and they could be found all over the system and not just on former LSWR lines. A few lingered on the mainland until after 1960 while those on the Island remained in constant use until electrification. The letter 'E' below the wagon number signifies Eastleigh and that the wagon was of LSWR origin.*

Bottom - *This one was a real surprise – a genuine former Somerset & Dorset Joint Railway wagon, as signified by the letter 'D' on the wagon plate under the number. Incidentally, the plate was rectangular – a chunk has broken off the lower right-hand corner at some stage, probably when someone took it off to reverse the plate when repainted from S&DJR to SR livery after 1930. The painting instruction for wagon plates reads: - "Cast iron number plate to be turned over, surface painted black and new number painted in white thereon in 2½ in white block figures with a 2in white block letter A, B, D or E beneath to denote place where wagon was built or at home". The subject matter is remarkable on two counts: one of only three ex-S&D wagons to feature and one of only two Engineer's Department wagons to be photographed, this was still so allocated in 1948 – and still to the S&D section to boot! It may be red oxide as this was the standard colour for ED stock at the time. No. s62948 began life as S&DJR no. 327 in 1903 and was one of fifty such vehicles retained by the Joint line for ballasting purposes in 1914, when most of the goods stock was divided between the LSWR and the Midland Railway, finally passing to the Southern in 1930. It appears to be in original condition, save for the addition of a second set of brake gear at some stage, to comply with Board of Trade regulations on either-side brake gear, which would not have applied when originally constructed. Withdrawal date is not known, but doubtless not long into the 1950s. No Southern Railway diagram number was officially allocated, but Diagram 1732, allocated to similar ex-Joint line dropside wagons inherited by the LSWR in 1914, would have sufficed. Despite the lack of a background, examination of the trackwork reveals that, given a few yards one way or the other, all three wagons were photographed at almost the same location.*

A Maunsell-era ex-SECR 13-ton open to Diagram 1355, no. s28951 was photographed in April 1948 – at a slightly different location within Ashford Works yard. One of 2121 wagons constructed to this Lionel Lynes design between 1915 and 1927, this example was actually completed by the Southern in February 1927 and was one of 1650 to remain in traffic at Nationalisation. It retains its sheet rail, while sister-wagon s16510, photographed at the same time, did not. Typical Lynes details are the heavy self-contained buffers (not unlike those used by the GWR at Swindon – Lynes' previous employer), the either-side brake gear with just two brake blocks acting on this side only but capable of operation from both sides, and the top doors – a feature also found on late LSWR open wagons. Notice behind are two ex-LBSCR wagons – to the right an open goods with a restricted-use branding and to the left, and more significant, a covered goods wagon. This tends to confirm that some wagon types were ignored; since no example of LBSCR van features in the series – yet here was one conveniently available for overhaul and photography. Open 28951 became a cable wagon in March 1952, serving as such until at least May 1965.

Ex-SECR stock			
SR Diagram	**Number**	**Description**	**Remarks**
1347	s14271	5-plank open goods	Unfitted
1347	s14422	5-plank open goods	Vacuum fitted
1349	s14590	5-plank open goods	
1355	s16510	7-plank open goods	
1355	s28951	7-plank open goods	SR built. With sheet rail
1424	s45374	Covered goods wagon	Wainwright design
1426	s45682	Covered goods wagon	Vacuum fitted
1426	s45757	Covered goods wagon	Unfitted
1427	s45618	Ventilated covered goods	Ex-diagram 1426

1515	s53589	Cattle wagon	Taken 10/48
1558	s55405	6w 20-ton goods brake van	Wainwright design
1560	s55489	25-ton goods brake van	"Dance hall"
1610	S58206/8	Twin bolster wagons	Permanently paired
1657	s60370	Road vehicle truck	Coded cartruck. Date 6/49
1703	s61236	Gunpowder van	Wainwright design

Total 15 vehicles. Some others extant in 1948 that were not included are the various RCH minerals and their derivatives, plus brake van diagram 1559.

This remarkable survivor was one of just five Wainwright SECR vans to Diagram 1424 to last into Nationalisation. No. s45374 was built at Ashford in March 1906, numbered SECR 9960 – one of 110 built between 1904 and 1908. With their outside timber framing, these were typical Wainwright vehicles and were an enlargement of a design that went back to the 1860s but equipped with more modern brakes and running gear. When built it had Hills either-side brake gear – one of a number of such patented brake gears used by many railways in the early years of the 20th century. Mr E. J. Hill was at the time a well-known consulting mechanical engineer with headquarters in Victoria Street, London. More conventional Freighter brakes (two independent sets of brakes on each side) were provided in May 1938 and the van was "extensively repaired", so the wagon register entry states, in April 1939. This clearly allowed survival through to 1948 and beyond, while the register also records that the van was specifically allocated to paper traffic between Aylesford and Blackfriars in July 1933 – not that there is anything on the van to indicate this in 1948. Surprisingly, it remained in traffic until 1956. The letter A below the wagon number signifies Ashford Works and SECR origin. This picture includes a full background looking towards Ashford town over the fence to the Kimberley wagon yard - the usual location for pre-war wagon photographs taken in those days by local photography firm De'Ath & Condon. By 1948 this arrangement had ceased and one presumes the railway's own staff were now in charge of the cameras.

10-ton van s45682 is perhaps more in keeping with 1948 rolling stock – this being a Lynes vehicle of 1918 to SR Diagram 1426 and very much the precursor of SR covered goods wagon designs. A total of 401 were completed between 1915 (the single "pattern" van) and 1926 – 101 being vacuum fitted as per this example. They featured 3-part "LNWR-type" doors (two cupboard doors over a drop flap), the characteristic Lynes semi-elliptical roof profile and a single end ventilator hood. Later SR vehicles were 6 inches longer at 17ft 6in, did not have the 3-part door and had two ventilators at each end but were recognisably from the same design parentage. Most were of 12 tons capacity but some were only 10 tons owing to the reuse of secondhand wheelsets and other fittings. Of the SECR version, 385 were still in ordinary traffic in 1948, including six that had been modified as Diagram 1427 and a few lasted beyond 1961. Almost all of the missing 16 vans had recently entered departmental stock in 1946-48. Van 45682 was withdrawn in 1955. Note a SECR "dance hall" brake van partially obliterated behind – almost certainly s55489 also pictured in the series.

Ex-LBSCR stock

SR Diagram	Number	Description	Remarks
1365/1368	s22045	5-plank open goods	Steel u/f and square ends
1364/1366	s19475	5-plank open goods	Timber u/f, square ends, uprated from 8 to 10 tons
1364/1369	s23682	5-plank open goods	Timber u/f, square ends
1576	s55915	20-ton goods brake van	Modern 1922 design

Total 4 vehicles. Some others extant in 1948 that were not included are the covered goods vans, cattle wagons, bolster wagons, other Panter brake vans and the road vehicle truck.

One of just four LBSCR wagons included in the series, this is Diagram 1364/1369 5-plank 10-ton open wagon s23682, photographed in the Kimberley yard in October 1948. It is also a rare picture where a member of staff (the shunter) has got in on the act! Built at Lancing in 1921 as LBSCR no. 5078, it originally had round ends and probably a sheet rail as well (Diagram 1369) in typical Brighton fashion but these were steadily removed from 1926 onwards so it should have been reallocated to Diagram 1364 – but despite the early start made on removal some wagons went for scrap in the early 1950s still so equipped. This was the Brighton's most numerous design and at least 3500 examples were built – plus a similar number with myriad variations in wheelbase, carrying capacity and other details but they all looked much the same. Many were sent to the Isle of Wight from 1924 onwards and these were, not surprisingly, the last survivors, some running until electrification. In contrast no. 23682 was withdrawn in 1952 and only a few departmental examples remained on the mainland after 1957. Less than 1600 wagons of this type remained in service in 1946 and this total was down to 1300 by nationalisation – about one third of these on the Isle of Wight and a good many of the mainland examples never received any form of British Railways livery or lettering before scrapping. Note the letter B on the wagon plate below the number – signifying Brighton and LBSCR origin. The Southern's mechanical engineering department hierarchy was not populated by many ex-LBSCR men after 1923 and the Brighton's products became regarded as non-standard at Eastleigh and Ashford – company bias one might say, but when it came to compliance with modern RCH standards, most ex-LBSCR wagons failed and their almost unique 6ft 3in wheelset journal spacing (and other factors, too) told against them. In the days before common user policies most would remain on their home metals where this was not a problem but by the 1920s with countrywide wagon distribution, repair at a far-flung location could be difficult. For this reason the Southern sent many to the Isle of Wight or transferred them to departmental service. Both options kept the wagons within a restricted geographical area as well as ensuring that annual mileages would be small, thereby reducing maintenance problems to manageable levels.

Southern Railway standard designs			
SR Diagram	**Number**	**Description**	**Remarks**
1375	s12134	13-ton 5-plank open	"Austerity" version
1375	s13474	13-ton 5-plank open	Post-war version
1377	s37815	13-ton 8-plank open	10ft wb, unfitted
1379	s36194	13-ton 8-plank open	Original 9ft wb design
1380	s10161	13-ton 5-plank open	Maunsell design
1381B	s26675	10-ton 8-plank open	With LSWR axleboxes
1382A	s39265	13-ton short container truck	Conflat B
1383	s39516	14-ton long container truck	Conflat D
1384	s40008	13-ton 7-plank mineral	RCH design

An 8-plank 13-ton open no. s36194 – an example of a Southern Railway standard wagon to Diagram 1379 – by a considerable margin the most numerous SR wagon diagram with no less than 7950 completed between 1926 and 1933. However, the SR 8-plank family actually included a further 3700 wagons with only slightly different details and allocated seven more diagrams. This wagon dates from 1931 and was still in service as recently as 1958. The picture was taken in April 1948 (this seems to have been when the vast majority of the series were taken) and shows a wagon still almost in original condition, save for very minor alterations to the way in which the timberwork was retained in place. The carrying capacity has also been raised by one ton during World War two. In this instance the background has been obscured but the position in Ashford yard appears little different to the other pictures. It looks like it was a wet day!

1386	s40610	21-ton 8-plank mineral	
1387	s36492	12-ton 8-plank open	Dover Ferry wagon
1388	s40983	21-ton 8-plank open	Dover Ferry wagon
1389	s38422	13-ton 5-plank open	Vacuum fitted
1390	s41281	13-ton 8-plank mineral	RCH design
1392	s14060	13-ton shock absorbing open	Taken 2/49 when new
		All-steel open	Later departmental 1429s
		All-steel mineral	All-steel mineral
Both the above were Bulleid experiments, were unpainted and did not enter traffic.			
1398	s37160	13-ton 8-plank open	10ft wb, vacuum fitted
1399	s39353	13-ton short container truck	Conflat S
1400	s10953	10-ton 8-plank open	Secondhand wheelsets

1428	s47261	12-ton covered goods	Unfitted
1428	s47911	12-ton covered goods	Vacuum fitted
1429	s44475	10-ton covered goods	With LSWR axleboxes
1429	s46919	10-ton covered goods	Vacuum fitted
1430	s47217	12-ton covered goods	Dover Ferry wagon
1452	s56830	12-ton covered goods	Plywood body
1455	s45259	12-ton covered goods	
1458	s48580	12-ton covered goods	Vacuum fitted
1459	s49091	12-ton covered goods	With internal partitions
1476	s50495	10-ton refrigerator van	Stone with red lettering
1477	s50561	11-ton insulated meat van	White with black lettering
1478	s50610	10-ton banana van	Bauxite livery (?)
1529	s53629	10-ton cattle wagon	Maunsell design
1530	s52429	10-ton cattle wagon	Bulleid design
1550	s56297	25-ton goods brake van	Standard SR design
1578	s55952	25-ton goods brake van	LH duckets, no sandboxes

The Southern completed just 12 shock-absorbing open wagons prior to nationalisation (allocated Diagram 1376) and none of these were photographed. A further batch of 38 was built at Ashford in early 1949, differing only in detail and allocated to Diagram 1392. No. s14060 was photographed when new in late February – the painting date of 21-2-49 appears on the solebar. This was a vacuum braked example; half of the batch were originally unfitted. Note that the wagon plate now proclaims BR and the date of 1948 – presumably when the underframe was completed – a month or two before bodywork and finishing. The paint finish includes the three white vertical stripes on both sides and ends to denote a shock-absorbing wagon. In later years guard plates were provided over the body movement control springs. Most of these wagons were allocated to specific duties and home stations, this information being recorded on the side planking and also on copies of the diagrams. No. 14060 was later allocated to Horsham, running into the 1970s.

1579	s56485	25-ton goods brake van	RH duckets, 2+2 planking
1580	s56269	28 ton bogie brake van	Rebuild of LBSC AC van
1581	s55722	15-ton goods brake van	Lighter version
1582	s55160	25-ton goods brake van	With revised brake rigging
1583	s55675	16-ton goods brake van	Cut down for C & W line
1681	s61056	21-ton machinery truck	Well B
1682	s61103	20-ton flatrol well wagon	Bulleid design
1691	s3	18-ton snowplough	Taken 12/48 when new
1749	Ds62682	20-ton plough brake van	ED stock red oxide

This last was probably photographed new in February 1949 rather than as part of the main series of illustrations.

Total 45 vehicles. There are a number of omissions, including vacuum fitted open diagram 1385, banana van diagram 1479, ventilated meat van diagram 1486, Folkestone Harbour incline brake diagram 1561, both bogie bolsters; diagrams 1598 and 1599 and the 40-ton bogie well diagram 1690.

Containers			
SR Diagram	**Number**	**Description**	**Remarks**
3005/3014	AF329S	Small insulated	Stone with red lettering
3011	K623S	Large furniture	Stone with red lettering?
3012	BM655S	Large fresh meat	
3002/3015	FX554S	Large insulated meat	Stone with red lettering
3026	BD1284S	Large general	
3027	A1362S	Small general	
3028	BK1328S	Large furniture	

These were taken at Eastleigh in September/October 1949 and appear to be the final pictures in the series. Quite a number of other SR container diagrams were still extant at the time, so maybe only a representative few were covered. No open containers were photographed.

Opposite - We now go from the ordinary to the esoteric. Not so much a goods wagon, more an item of service stock allocated to the loco running department, this is snowplough S3, photographed (unusually) in broadside mode in The Klondike yard at Ashford when new in December 1948. However, it was finished in wagon brown livery. Four of these unusual vehicles (nos. S1-S4) were built – two in 1929 and two more in 1948 – both sets of construction being preceded by hard winters! They were allocated to strategic loco. sheds for use as required – which usually meant the west country and east Kent in addition to Basingstoke and Eastleigh. The vehicle is double-ended and by means of the lifting beam which has yet to be fitted at the top, between two of the brackets, the headstock/dumb buffer assembly may be raised or lowered – both seen raised in this instance. The beam may be swung round to deal with the other end, depending on the direction of travel. The usual mode of operation was to propel the wagon with headstock at leading end lowered, so presenting a smooth plough to the snow, the loco engaging with the coupling hook and raised headstock at the other end. It had been thought that this was a Lionel Lynes design, but recent correspondence with a member of the North Eastern Railway Society yields the fact that the NER had several practically identical vehicles from 1919 onwards. They would have had to deal with snow annually in their home area, so perhaps the design was "cribbed" by Ashford ten years later. Or maybe some inter-company co-operation for what, to the Southern, would be an essential vehicle but one not required very often so do not spend too long designing it. Why reinvent the wheel, etc? The cross-shaped handbrake "wheel" is noteworthy. Withdrawal dates are not known but some new ploughs were constructed on former "Schools" class tender underframes in 1964 (again after a hard winter!) and presumably these took over the duties.

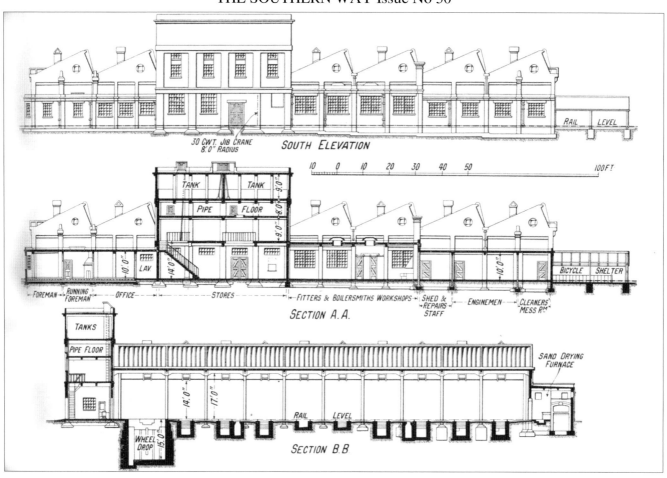

SOUTH ELEVATION

30 CWT. JIB CRANE
8'0" RADIUS

SECTION A.A.

FOREMAN · RUNNING FOREMAN · OFFICE · STORES · FITTERS & BOILERSMITHS WORKSHOPS · SHED & REPAIRS STAFF · ENGINEMEN · CLEANERS' MESS RM

TANK · TANK · PIPE FLOOR · LAV · RAIL LEVEL · BICYCLE SHELTER

SECTION B.B.

TANKS · PIPE FLOOR · WHEEL DROP · RAIL LEVEL · SAND DRYING FURNACE

From 'The Railway Gazette': 21 August 1931.

New Locomotive Depot at Ashford, Kent, Southern Railway

'A Noteworthy Feature of Construction is that the new Engine Shed and Coaling Stage are built entirely of reinforced Concrete.'

Prior to the recent completion and opening of the new locomotive depot of the Southern Railway at Ashford, Kent, the facilities for housing, coaling, watering, and maintaining locomotives at this important centre had become in the course of time somewhat outgrown, owing to the development of traffic and the increasing number of engines necessary for working the services for which demands are made upon Ashford for locomotive power. The original running shed, situated on the south side of the main line from London to Folkestone and Dover and adjoining the site of the locomotive carriage and wagon works of the original South Eastern Railway, had accommodation for only 15 or 16 engines. The new locomotive depot is situated about a quarter of a mile south-east of Ashford station in the fork of the junction of the Ashford to Ramsgate branch and the main London to Dover line. It represents an excellent example of modern building construction, and not only the running shed and other buildings, but also the layout of the yard, with its ample lighting, watering, and pit arrangements, are such as to facilitate greatly the movement of engines and expedite their handing in and out of traffic.

Work was commenced in November 1929, and the new engine shed, which, as already stated, is of reinforced concrete, provides accommodation for 35 to 40 locomotives, according to type and size. These can be accepted on 10 pit roads, which latter are placed 15 ft. apart and measure 260 ft. overall in length. The steam shed itself covers an area of 37,000 sq. ft., and the building in its complete form includes mess rooms for enginemen, cleaners, and repair staff, as well as office accommodation for the locomotive foreman. A feature of this office, which is situated at the north-west end of the shed, is the ample view obtained of the approach roads, the coaling stage, and a considerable portion of the shed itself. The staff buildings on this side of the shed also include a large workshop and stores accommodation, the latter on two floors, the building being surmounted by a concrete water tank in two sections with a total capacity of 54,000 gallons. On the east side of the building there is, in addition to a tool store, a sand drying furnace, whilst at the back of the shed, lavatory and washing accommodation is provided for the staff.

Track Layout

The locomotive shed is approached from a point opposite the 'E' signal cabin at a point approximately 200 yards from where the Ramsgate branch joins the main line. The layout of the tracks and the arrangements for getting engines to and from the shed, coaling stage, and water columns are illustrated below and opposite.

A single turnout from the down Ramsgate line

Left - General view of approach roads to shed looking north, and including turntable and coaling stage.

Opposite top - Side elevation and sections through workshops, stores and staff rooms and engine pits.

Opposite bottom - The yard looking south-east, and showing the turntable, coaling stage and shed approach roads.

eventually provided a fan-shaped access to the whole of the east side of the yard, including the coal stage, whilst a similar connection from the up Ramsgate line leads to the turntable and shed roads. All these tracks are ballasted on 2 ft. of ashes, and a system of drainage disposes of surface water into a stream which forms the east boundary of the company's property. The soiled water from the engine pit is led through a purification plant situated near the shed.

The system of layout is such that an engine can be cleaned, refuelled, and turned with a minimum of shunting. By means of a crossover road it is possible for an engine to proceed directly to the turntable, whence it can either be shunted into any one of the shed roads, or despatched for a

duty. The approach to the coal stage is on a tipped bank with a 1 in 30 gradient. The gradient itself rises from rail level in the yard to a height of approximately 12 ft., and it is continued at this level for a distance of 200 ft. beyond the coal stage, ample accommodation being thus provided for the coal wagons. These latter are pushed up the grade by locomotive power, passing over the coal stage proper and out beyond. This allows for a number of wagons being located at the higher level at one time, and after being emptied they return by gravity to the lower end of the 1 in 30 gradient. A sand drag and a catch are provided, thus preventing any danger of runaway vehicles.

Erection Methods.

In erecting the locomotive shed, special measures were resorted to, of which the following is a brief description. Apart from the walls and tank house, the whole of the superstructure, including the columns was pre-cast and erected by crane. In order to carry out this work satisfactorily it was necessary to obtain access to the whole length of the shed by rail, and with this object in view the pits were first constructed and the back and side walls cast *in situ*. At this stage, however, the work was by no means confined to the site of the shed. In addition to the pits and walls a large area outside had been transformed into a pre-casting ground, and each day marked the completion of various units such as columns, roof trusses, and purlins. The concrete consisted of a mixture of 4 of crushed gravel and 2 of clean sand to 1 of cement.

The columns were first dealt with, and altogether 110 of these were pre-cast. Those situated between each track measure 12 in. by 12 in., reinforced with four ¾-in. bars and a 3/16 i. links numbering 63 in all. Cast 19 ft. in length, they each have to carry the ends of the roof trusses in one direction and the ends of two gutter beams in the other. The remaining columns on the outside of the shed vary in size from 18 in. by 15 in. 24 in. by 15 in. and carry the gable trusses. The weight of each ordinary truss and each gable truss is 22 cwt. and 27 cwt. respectively, and they are built to resist a wind pressure of 30 lb. per sq. ft. There are 72 ordinary trusses in the shed and 14 gables.

The smoke troughs form the most interesting

Opposite page, top - The coaling stage.

Opposite page, centre - Interior of shed showing concrete roof columns and smoke troughs.

Opposite page, bottom - Entrance to shed looking south.

This page, top - Interior of tank building showing supplementary stores floor.

This page, centre - Water purification plant, showing sludge valve and pump.

This page, bottom - General view of roof showing smoke stacks.

(Text, captions and illustrations reproduced with grateful thanks from The Railway Gazette.)

part of the pre-cast constructional work. Owing to the fact that the sides are only 1¼ in. in thickness, a specially graded ballast was used. These troughs are reinforced with 1/8-in. perforated strip metal and were cast in Ciment Fondu in order to resist the injurious effect of sulphur fumes. In spite of their apparent frailness, no difficulty was found in lifting them into position 48 hours after they had been completed. The reception of pre-cast work was finished when the smoke troughs were in position and the square slabs 2 in. thick had been laid on the roof.

The roof itself is formed in a series of gables with north lighting, and is covered with a 1/8-in. layer of 'Masticon' to ensure a watertight condition, and this work, together with the glazing, completed the whole of the super-structure. The photographs of the roof reproduced shows the arrangement of the smoke stacks, or vents, communicating with the smoke troughs inside the shed.

An outstanding feature of the locomotive shed is the tank house, which rises to a height of 40 ft. above rail level. In addition to the ground or stores floor, there are two other floors before reaching the tank itself. The first of these is for supplementary stores and the second is a pipe floor from which the supply of water to all parts of the shed is regulated. The water is pumped from the company's reservoir. The tank itself is divided into two sections by a 5 in. concrete wall, and each section is capable of holding 27,000 gallons. They are lined with ¾-in. asphalt to form watertight compartments. Asphalt was also used on all flat roofs as well as in the gutters.

The floor of the shed was left until the end of the works, as it was not deemed advisable to attempt the formation of a good surface while there was the possibility of settlement. No difficulty, however, was found in making a good floor 6 in. in depth with a 6 to 1 mixture of ballast and cement. Whilst work on the floor was in hand the equipment for an electric wheel drop was installed. This is situated in the shed on the southernmost side. The track extending beyond the back of the shed enables an engine after leaving the wheel drop to pass on to the adjacent track by means of a crossover, thus leaving the wheel drop free for use in connection with another locomotive. The construction of the shed occupied 18 months, the work being completed throughout and handed over for traffic on June 13.

The lighting of the shed is excellent, both during the daytime and after dark. The building is well ventilated, and the arrangements made for the comfort and convenience of the staff both in the offices and other sections are admirable. The layout of the buildings, including a machine shop on the west side of the shed is shown on the plan drawing reproduced. The yard outside, provided with pits and water columns independent of those in the locomotive shed, is also excellently lighted, and our observations showed that all locomotive movements and preparations were being carried out in a smooth and uninterrupted manner, The addition of facilities of this kind has naturally reacted very considerably upon the conduct of traffic in the district.

The contractors for the running shed and coaling stage were Rice & Son Ltd., of Margate, and the electric wheel drop was supplied by Ransomes & Rapier Limited, of Ipswich.

We are indebted to Mr G Ellson, O.B.E., M.Inst.C.E., Chief Engineer, Southern Railway, for the above information and the drawings reproduced herewith, and also for facilities for visiting the depot.

Entrance to the shed showing foreman's office and tank house.

The last of the Ashford 'C's.

Photographs by David Hammersley

Top - 'C' class 0-6-0 No 592 is standing in Ashford Locomotive Works yard in front of the erecting shop. Recently purchased by the 'C' class Preservation Society, restoration has taken place in the open air. Just out of picture to the left is former works shunter, USA 0-6-0T No DS238 'Wainwright' and behind her is No DS239 'Maunsell'.

Right - On the same day No 592 was transferred to the Kimberley Wagon Works on the opposite side of the Ashford to Hastings line. On the left are the remains of an ex SEC brake van while in the sidings are two 'Thumper' DEMUs for the Hastings line, themselves now heritage stock.

This page - In the sidings at the far end of the wagon works was No DS240, formerly No 31271, recently withdrawn from heating boiler duties. Surrounded by platforms, ladders, pipes, piles of kindling and general works leftovers, she made a sorry sight.

Opposite page - No DS240 did do her bit for preservation as many fittings were recovered before the scrap man arrived. Moments after this picture was taken the chimney was levered off to bounce safely on a carpet of carriage cushions.

THE LAST OF THE ASHFORD 'C's.

No 592 carried on her restoration in the relative comfort of the Kimberley workshops. There was still work going on around her, but not for much longer. Later moving to the Ashford Steam centre in the former loco shed, her final home was the Bluebell Railway, where she has recently been transferred to the ownership of the Bluebell Railway Trust.
(With the exception of the bottom image on p59 which was recorded on 20 August 1967, all views were taken on 15 July 1967.)

Opposite page - TAKE 2 - and a bit.

Top - *Arrived just too late for inclusion in 'Twickenham Take 2' (SW29) was this view of the new station at Twickenham which opened on 28 March 1954.*

Bottom - *Another late arrival which would similarly have fitted in very well with the ongoing series on the History of the Southern Railway. Q1 No C40 is leaving Woking on a down freight for the Guildford line, 16 September 1940. B Butt.*

The Netley branch opened in 1866 from a junction at St Denys. It was extended to Fareham in 1876 and doubled in stages. **Woolston** station has the same Italianate style as St Denys, seen here with an eastbound L&SWR train. Located a few hundred yards from the Supermarine base, passengers for the seaplanes could alight here. Alternatively, they might prefer Southampton Terminus for a night in the South Western Hotel and a taxi across the floating bridge. There again, one might just drive down in the bull-nose Morris Oxford. Flying in those days was for the affluent. © *Lens of Sutton Association.*

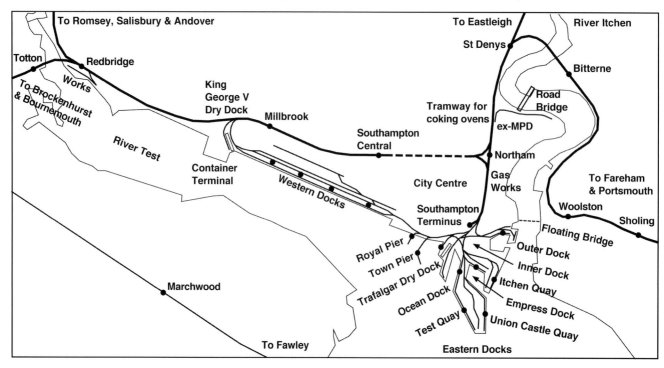

A Survey of Southampton's Railways
Part 1: Woolston to Redbridge

Alan Postlethwaite

Founded in 1913, **Woolston** was the HQ and works
of Supermarine, manufacturers of sea and land
planes. Spitfires were made here before being
transferred to a new larger factory at Castle
Bromwich. The first seaplane services operated for a
short while in 1919 from Woolston to le Havre.
During 1923-29, the British Marine Air Navigation
Company operated flying boats from Woolston to
Guernsey and Cherbourg with through bookings
undertaken by the Southern Railway. This merged
into Imperial Airways in 1924 which became part of
BOAC. Supermarine became a subsidiary of Vickers
-Armstrong in 1928 and the Woolston works became
defunct after bombing in 1940. The top picture
shows the Supermarine works, railway line and
floating bridge. The RH picture shows an amphibian
Sea Otter alongside the works. In 1933, the Big Four
and Imperial founded Railway Air Services to
operate domestic routes with land and sea planes.
Part 2 of this article will show some larger
international flying boats which operated pre- and
post-war from the Eastern and Western Docks.
Provenance unknown (both)

Introduction

I first photographed Southampton's railways and docks in 1958. When researching another Southern Way article on *Southern Coal*, I became intrigued by Northam MPD which had disappeared without trace. I felt compelled to make a field visit to see what was left of Southampton's railways. It became the genesis of this article.

Southampton's railways and docks are already covered in six superb pictorial histories by Bert Moody, Ian Drummond and Dave Marden. They are pretty thorough - so how does one justify a fresh magazine article? The answer is to review what has gone before, to fill a few gaps and to use predominantly different illustrations. There are also certain key pictures that are worth repeating. The result is a lively introduction to Southampton's railway history using a wealth of illustrations not previously published.

A lot of new material is available these days on line but whose provenance has been lost in the mists of time. Despite best efforts to trace the owners, if I have included any untraced picture whose copyright owner is still around, then please get in touch.

Bitterne Station.

Opposite, top - Simple facilities and grassy platforms at **Sholing**. The village became part of Southampton in 1920. Class 4MT No. 75070 heads east with the RCTS 'Solent Rail Tour' a long train, on 20 March 1966. *Tony Molyneaux.*

Opposite, bottom - **Bitterne** was given substantial brick buildings. The grounded four-wheel L&SWR 3rd class coach has an extremely low arc roof, almost flat. It is being used here for light goods storage. The warren girder footbridge is characteristic of the L&SWR and survives to this day. *© Lens of Sutton Association*

Above - An unidentified Schools class heads the Up 'Union Castle Express' through **St Denys**. The building has strong Italianate architecture. Opened in 1864 to serve the Netley branch, it replaced Portswood station just to the north and was renamed in 1876. *AFP/ © Bluebell 1958*

Above - The Hampshire DEMUs were introduced in 1957 for local passenger services. The lines though Southampton were electrified in 1967 but the line to Fareham remained diesel operated until 1990. Unit 1126 is standing in Platform 4 at **St Denys** when engineering work was on-going. It is about to return to Portsmouth, hence the red blind. *© Malcolm Best, RPA 1975*

In the glorious days of semaphore signalling, the Down Starter array at **St Denys** was majestic. The provisions shown here are from three eras:

Opposite, top: - Two dissimilar L&SWR brackets, possibly recycled from elsewhere, survived into BR days. The pairs of ringed auxiliaries were for entry into Bevois Park goods yard, just beyond the road bridge. This yard served industries including motor spirit, cement, car transport and gun carriage manufacture during the First World War. © *John Bailey/ SCRS 1955*

Opposite, bottom - This BR gantry was installed in 1955. Less tall, sturdier (with no sway) and without co-acting arms, it is no less imposing than its predecessors. © *Malcolm Best/ RPA 1975*

This page, top - Colour lights were installed in 1981 - signals in a nutshell. The 'flying banana' is not a Sprinter but a unique track inspection DEMU called Euro-Scout or the Southern Measurement Train (SMT) of Network Rail. Made in Austria by Plasser & Theurer, it is en route here from Totton to Willesden via Fareham. © *Malcolm Best/ RPA 2006*

The Up approach trackwork to **St Denys** was also developed in stages:

Middle - When the main line south of St Denys was quadrupled from 1901, the Down lines were given four junction points but the Up lines only two plus a sand drag. The L&SWR Type 4 signal box was connected at the back directly to the gatekeeper's cottage. *JJS/ © Bluebell 1966*

Bottom - In 1975, the junction was rebuilt with six points (and no sand drag) for the Up trains and incorporated a facing crossover for entry into Bevois Park yard. All running lines through Southampton became reversible in 1981. Express Sprinter No. 158881 is en route from Romsey to Salisbury via Eastleigh and Redbridge. © *Bob Foster 2008*

Approaching **Mount Pleasant** crossing, LNER class A3 No. 4472 *Flying Scotsman* heads the Greater Manchester Railway Society 'Isle of Wight Special' back to Lincoln. The goods sidings on the left are on the site of Northam MPD which closed in 1903 when Eastleigh opened. There were once coking ovens there for the very first L&SWR locomotives, with coal delivered from the Itchen by the Northam Wharf Tramway. The MPD had a 15-road shed. The goods yard became a Blue Circle Cement depot and the site is now the Siemens Traincare Facility for EMU servicing. *JJS/ © Bluebell 1963*

Serving mainly industrial workers, **Northam**'s platform buildings were unprepossessing. With plentiful issues of steam, class N15 No. 30789 *Sir Guy* heads an Up train with an LNER bogie luggage van at the front. *AFP/ © Bluebell 1958*

South of Mount Pleasant, the railway resembles a Scalextric race track with four main lines, two freight lines and multiple goods sidings. **Northam Junction**'s Down Home signal gantry was a monster. Most of the auxiliary arms were for exit from Northam marshalling yard onto the running lines to Central station, the Terminus and docks. Just passing with the 11.22 a.m. Waterloo to Bournemouth is class LN No. 30860 *Lord Hawke*. © *Tony Molyneaux 28 September 1957*

Class 4MT No. 76017 simmers gently on a freight line by **Northam** station. The gas works site beyond has since been redeveloped as St Mary's football stadium, opening in 2001. From just north of here, the private Chapel Tramway ran to Belvidere and James wharves on the Itchen, closing in 1967. From just south of here, the private Bull's Run Siding ran to Britannia, Phoenix, Burnley, Victoria, Sunderland, Union and Dibbles wharves, closing in 1989. Dibbles Wharf became a major coal depot, serving much of Hampshire as well as the Tramways power station. *AFP/ © Bluebell 1958*

Opposite, top - **Tunnel Junction** was three-quarters of a mile from Southampton Terminus. Northam station can be seen below the gas holder. Built in 1861, the signal box is an exceptionally tall L&SWR Type 1 with replacement windows. When it closed in 1966, it was one of the oldest surviving L&SWR boxes. *JJS/ © Bluebell 1966*

Opposite, bottom - Photographed from **Tunnel Junction** signal box, class WC No. 34105 *Swanage* heads the 10.05 am Southampton to Waterloo along the canyon from Southampton tunnel. The house backs and garden sheds were built awfully close to the smokey canyon. Note the signal bracket with co-acting arms - as tall as the three-storey houses. © *Tony Molyneaux 28 September 1957.*

Below - The north curve of the **Northam Triangle** opened in 1858. Light Pacific No. 34098 *Templecombe* shaves the houses with a train to Waterloo. Historic advertisements are for EKCO television and Strong's Golden Ale - reminiscent of the Strong Country hoardings by the West of England main line. Knight's Foot Clinic is no more - indeed, most of the shops in that row are now empty. Note the cabbages by the lineside and the washing in the distant back yard. *AFP/ © Bluebell 1958*

The line through the city centre was awkward with tight curves, a canyon between the backs of buildings and a tunnel which bisected an earlier canal tunnel. One section of the tunnel collapsed during construction and another section caused subsidence and the demolition of alms houses. The tunnel was part bore and part cut-and-cover.

The original route sought by the Southampton and Dorchester Railway Company would have gone along the waterfront from the Terminus but the Harbour Commissioners objected to steam locomotives on the waterfront. Indeed, traffic along Canute Road remained horse-drawn with wagon turntables until 1876.

Our journey will now progress through the tunnel to Central station and beyond. The Terminus and Docks will be covered in Part 2 of this article in issue No 31 of *The Southern Way.*

Left - **Northam Junction** signal box had several types of train describer. *JJS/ © Bluebell 1965*

Opposite—Pick your favourite pre-Grouper as two Drummonds and a Brighton Atlantic pass beneath an impressive array of Down Starter signals at **Southampton Central**:

Top - Drummond 'Greyhound' class T9 No. 30732 was built in 1899. *CH/ © Bluebell 1953*

Middle - Drummond's final class D15 No. 30464 was built in 1912. *CH/ © Bluebell 1952*

Bottom - Marsh/ Billinton class H2 No. 32426 *St Albans Head* was built in 1912. It heads a through service from Brighton to Bournemouth. *CH/ © Bluebell ca 1952*

At **Southampton Junction**, a class 33 (alias D65xx) brings a train of banana vans off the south curve of the Northam triangle which opened in 1847. Beyond is Northam station which opened in 1871 originally for ticket collection in the days of non-corridor trains. The road bridge beyond was rebuilt for trams in 1908 using great steel trusses. They cross the lines at a skew to Central station (left) and to the Terminus and docks (below). © *John H. Bird/ RailwayImages.com 1967*

Between the tunnel mouth and **Central station**, class 3MT tank No. 82015 stands on a siding used formerly to transfer coal wagons across the road to the Corporation's power station. This opened in 1904 primarily to power the trams. A branch of Babies R Us stands on the power station site today. Where the siding joins the main line is the site of the first railway station here called Blechynden, later renamed Southampton West. This opened in 1847 and was superseded in 1895 by a larger station just beyond, now known as Southampton Central. The odd-looking power station steel chimney tapers the wrong way for the efficient dispersal of gases. © *Tony Molyneaux 1955*

The Down buildings of **Central station** were rebuilt in 1935 in art-deco Odeon style. The rectangular block sticking out in the middle is a 1980 rebuild of the booking office which was bombed in 1941. In 2012, a new entrance and booking hall were opened at the east end of the suite in the former SR buffet and bar. Parcels offices are at the far end. © *AFP 2014*

Top - **Southampton Central**'s original buildings were in Queen Anne style and included an iconic clock tower. In an act of corporate vandalism which John Betjeman would surely have condemned, the Up buildings and tower were replaced in 1988 by a square monolith of offices with the railway facilities tucked below. The Down buildings were also in Queen Anne style until rebuilding in 1935. In this scene, the two Up trains are headed by class N15 No. 30790 *Sir Villiars* and class WC No. 34094 *Mortehoe*. © *Tony Molyneaux 1956*

Bottom - **Southampton Central** got a new signal box in 1935 when the station was expanded from two to four through platforms and the line was quadrupled as far as Millbrook. It is in the 'modern style' initiated by London Transport and perpetuated by the Big Four. Southern characteristics are the flat roof, locking room extensions and a central band of concrete which carries the name. Its bland squareness was not to everybody's liking. It is surprising that it was not given the more rounded and pleasing-to-the-eye Odeon style given to the new Down station buildings in the same year. The passing locomotive here is class 4MT No.75078. © *Tony Molyneaux 1956*

Opposite, top - When the line from Central station was expanded to four tracks in 1935, **Millbrook** lost its up platform and the down platform became an island. On the down avoiding line, class U No. 31808 heads an Andover train with a set of early Bulleid corridor stock which has extra doors. The RH tracks are to/ from the Western Docks. In 1968, Millbrook's goods yard was rebuilt as a Freightliner Terminal. The Maritime Container Port followed in 1972. © *Tony Molyneaux 1956*

Headed by class Q No. 30542 and class 4MT No. 76064, a train of Redbridge track sections approaches **Millbrook**. The single line on the left is a remnant of the wartime western connection to the Western Docks. © *Tony Molyneaux 1959*

Class 700 'Black Motors' were once commonplace on freight throughout the L&SWR. No 30316 is assisting at **Millbrook** with the recovery of a derailed train. The extreme LH signal is for entry to the Western Docks. © *Tony Molyneaux 1958*

Middle - Approaching **Millbrook**, class U No. 31802 heads a mixed freight from Salisbury. The ESSO tank wagons may be destined for the Fawley refinery via Millbrook yard. © *Tony Molyneaux 2 August 1958*

Bottom - The L&SWR's Permanent Way Works at **Redbridge** opened in 1881. Sleepers were imported at its wharf. They were then seasoned, dried, machined and impregnated with creosote. The works subsequently expanded to produce castings, concrete sleepers, long-welded rail and pre-assembled track. The works closed in 1989. With some eight miles of sidings, shunting was done successively by horse, steam crane, B4 tank, C14 tank, O2 tank, USA tank, and diesel classes 07 and 08, represented here by No. 08030. © *Malcolm Best 1979*

Approaching **Redbridge** across the marshy River Test, LNER class V2 No. 60908 heads a Bournemouth train to Waterloo. The V2s were temporary replacements for the troublesome Bulleid Merchant Navy Pacifics. *JJS/ © Bluebell 1953*

Departing **Millbrook**, class M7 tank No. 30377 heads a train of GWR stock to Fawley. The signal box is in the same 'modern style' as Southampton Central. The curves on the right lead to the Western Docks, forming a long loop to Southampton Terminus. The GWR stock is explained by using coaches off a Didcot - Newbury working which would otherwise have stood idle at Southampton Terminus. © *Tony Molyneaux 2 August 1958*

References
Moody, Bert, *Southampton's Railways*, Atlantic Publishers, 1992.
Drummond, Ian, *Southern Rails around Southampton including the Fawley Branch*, Holne Publishing, 2011.
Mitchell, Vic and **Smith**, Keith, 3 volumes in the Middleton Press series: *Portsmouth to Southampton* (1986); *Southampton to Bournemouth* (1987); and *Woking to Southampton* (1988).
Fairman, JR, *Making Tracks*, Kingfisher Railway Productions, 1988.
Fagan, Dave, *Southampton Flying Boat Services 1919-1958*, Hampshire Airfields website.
Stroud, John, *Railway Air Services*, Ian Allan, 1987.
Catford, Nick, *Disused Stations* website.

Abbreviated Credits
Photographers, Collections and Copyright Owners:

AFP   Alan Postlethwaite
Bluebell   Bluebell Railway Photographic Archive
CH   Colin Hogg
JJS   John J. Smith
RPA   Rail Photographic Archive
SCRS   Southern Counties Railway Society

Another large number of topics in a bulging postbag—thank you, and keep it coming! First from Eric Youldon, "In reply to Mr C Sayers Merchant Navy coupling rods notes on page 91 of SW28, I can confirm that at least 22 of the class were given plain rods before rebuilding. The Pacific quoted, No 35016, received them in September 1956 before rebuilding in 1957. It is interesting to recall the photographs on p68 of SW11 that showed a fractured coupling rod on rebuilt MN 35021 at Winchester. Your correspondent's suggestion regarding steel quality would appear to be justified. All 'light Pacifics' retained fluted coupling rods to withdrawal.

I had no sooner penned my notes on MN coupling rods when I read Tony Carter's query asking when did the GWR abandon its large page passenger time table for the small fat format. The answer is the final large page issue was for Winter 1947-48. The first small issue was therefore the BR(WR) book for summer 1948. As I write this I have both copies in front of me. A further change in page size occurred in mid 1955 when the Passenger Time Table for all regions enjoyed a useful increase in page size resulting in what was undoubtedly the handiest version thus far."

Now from Mike Green, "Just a couple of points which are probably completely out of date now. (Not at all, the whole idea is be bring to light new information {and as you will see the editor's omissions], even if from some time past - Ed). Southern Way 23: In the article about Somerset Peat Railways it shows two pictures on p59 and p60 captioned as the crossing of the S&D. The correct one is obviously p60. Southern Way 24: on p43 it states in the caption that 30062 was not known to be on an RCTS trip. It

was though on a rail tour on 12/5/53 which would fit in with the time that Tony Carter went to work at Southampton. Could this be a photo of that trip?

Mike also correctly points out an unintended omission where we failed to state what is the obvious, (NEVER assume anything-Ed). "In SW25 it states that the branch to Hurstbourne closed in 1931, it didn't. It was the passenger service that ceased in July 1931 although the line stayed open for local goods to Wherwell and Longparish, and the occasional diverted goods train from the Basingstoke to Southampton line until severed north of Longparish at the A303 Road bridge in May 1934. After this a local goods train continued to serve the two stations from the Fullerton Junction end until October 1942 when more sidings were put in at Fullerton and Longparish to serve the bomb dumps in Harewood Forest and therefore traffic was much increased. These dumps were largely cleared between 1945 and 1950 but the local goods continued for a few more years until the last one ran on the 28 May 1956 pulled by T9 30288. The line was then used for wagon storage and later EMU storage. The new Hampshire DEMUs were also tested on it in 1957. It was officially taken out of use 20 April 1960. There are references to the line in the books by Ed Goodwich, Nigel Bray, Vic Mitchell and Keith Smith and Peter Harding."

Now from Mike King, "A few comments regarding the articles: 'Southern Freight Contrasts', the first order for the Z class tanks was No B189 dated 27 July 1926, for construction at Brighton (so which show the allocated running numbers as B950-957!), intended for completion by 30 June 1928, so it seems they were required with some

Winter at Whitton, 27 February 1946.

Cab and injector detail of S15 No 30510.

urgency - in the event the order was not actually completed and closed until 9/29. The second order was No E564, placed on 8 April 1930 but cancelled on 27 March 1931. This time no running numbers were allocated but it would be reasonable to assume these would be Nos. 958-967.

"The next order, this time for the W class followed on immediately as No E565, yet oddly the order for the final ten pre-dated this one as No E501, dated 18 July 1929. A later entry, order No A834 dated 31st October 1934 covered the production of ten boilers for the class - so presumably the trade depression of the early 1930s caused the SR Board to defer construction or at least to restrict work to just assemblage of materials. Order E501 was subsequently transferred to Ashford.

"The wagon behind Z class No 954 on p10 (SW28), is indeed a shunter's truck - in fact the solitary LSWR example, SR No 61321 - and a long-term resident of Exmouth Junction yards, which is where the photograph was taken, probably not so long after No. 954 was completed as the loco still carries its 'A' prefix over the number. So we have probably the unique situation of a Southern class that was allocated numbers first in the Brighton sequence, then the Ashford sequence, but finally remained in the Eastleigh series without renumbering in either the 1000 or 2000 blocks!

"Now to Midhurst - the picture of Pull-Push fitted M7 No 54 is interesting as the loco is coupled to a pair of LSWR 56ft corridor brake composite coaches - most definitely not pull-push fitted - and probably a fairly unusual sight at the location. The other branch photographs show the more usual LSWR or LBSCR pull-push coaches

or sets. LBSCR Balloon PP coaches were also seen there, often coupled to an M7 on the Petersfield working.

"The accident at Clapham Junction showing downrated LSWR thirds Nos 164 and 166 spelt the end for recently formed West London line set No 410. This had appeared around early 1956 formed of brake thirds 2608 and 2613, with former composites (now thirds/seconds) 164, 166, 168 and composite 4751 between them - all six being LSWR rebuilt bodies on standard SR 58ft underframes. Not surprisingly, withdrawal of all six coaches is recorded as July 1957.

"And finally 'The Grid'. I corresponded regularly with Ray Tustin in the 1970s and 80s and he recounted some further memories of the working. All the time the LSWR 4-coach bogie block sets were on suburban duties, these were the regular stock - and there were usually plenty of different ones from which to choose. However, between 1928 and 1930 these were all withdrawn for conversion to electric vehicles and , according to Ray, on one memorable day the matter of stock for 'The Grid' must have been overlooked. Instead of the usual formation, all that arrived was a LSWR 48ft 8-compartment third and a six-wheeled passenger brake van. He recalls the journey that day was overcrowded to put it mildly! The hasty replacement and what became the permanent one, was LBSCR arc-roofed 3-set No 799, formed of brake thirds Nos 3940 and 3950 with composite No 6124 in the centre. One wonders who used the first class compartments - prefects and sixth formers maybe, or was it a free for all, or did they even keep these particular compartments locked? The set served until May 1936, after which another LBSCR set was substituted until the duty ceased. About a dozen such LBSCR sets were allocated to the South Western section after about 1932 and could be seen as far away as Plymouth, Torrington, Barnstaple, Exeter, Southampton, Eastleigh and Bournemouth that is until their final demise around 1940. This may have been the only one in the SW London area. Ray also mentioned that all five of the H16 tanks did a turn on the working - conveniently obliging the number collecting fraternity."

Still on the subject of 'Southern Goods Workings' and relating to the photograph on p11, from Tony Francis, Fleet Standards Engineer, Southern Railway. "Useless info department, (absolutely not-Ed), but the picture on page 11 of the above article which shows a W Class at Factory Junction, must have been taken circa 1953/54. The reason, in the background, Battersea Power Station is in the course of an extension to add the 'B' portion to the East of the pre-war 'A' station. As can be seen, the South East chimney has yet to be constructed and as the 'B' part of the station opened in 1955 this view must have been taken at some point before that."

Continuing with 'the Grid', from Nick Stanbury, "Having lived by Fulwell Station on the Shepperton line, I was well aware of 'The Grid' steam service for pupils of Hampton Grammar School, albeit that it ceased in 1939, well before my residency (1949-73). I can add a little to John Burgess's interesting article in SW28, partially gleaned from the souvenir programme issued for the Hampton Transport Gala on 7 September 2014, marking the 150th anniversary of the station and the branch. The programme includes the photo of M7 No 25 on the service and suggests that a T9 was sometimes used instead.

"The School relocated in 1939 from near Hampton Station to its present premises in a more remote area (and which dissuaded me from attending when I came to choose a grammar school). The School is about a 15 minute walk away from Hampton Station and was no nearer to the trolleybus route (667), although served sporadically by other buses. My understanding is that 'The Grid' ran between Richmond (rather than Twickenham) and Hampton morning, lunchtime and afternoon. This is surprising, as Richmond would have been less convenient operationally and I doubt that it produced many pupils – being 'out of county' in Surrey whilst the School was funded by Middlesex County Council. Perhaps some boys came from further away in Middlesex via the District or LMS services – the opposite of my own school journey to Hammersmith. Even more surprising was the lunchtime return working (a 15 minute run to Richmond), which could hardly have given time for even Twickenham boys to reach home, have lunch and catch the return service. Or did some pupils attend only for half a day?

"As to the last Southern steam-hauled passenger service 'regularly running over electrified lines', I am doubtful that this was 'The Grid'. It depends what one means by 'regular' – my view being 'established and repeated', if not necessarily frequent and in the public timetable. Interestingly, I can think of some others on the Shepperton line, which saw a number of wartime steam-hauled trains taking POWs to and from a camp at Kempton Park race course. Also, in (I think) October 1958, flooding in and around Fulwell station (still a problem today) caused the electric service between Teddington and Hampton to be replaced by a steam shuttle for two or three days. I watched these trains and would love to see some details and photos if anyone has them; one was filmed and shown on the BBC news. *(Any offer please? Ed.)* Further afield, there were other lines on which steam trains ran temporarily (but to a timetable) during disruption of the electric service (e.g. through flooding – Clock House comes to mind – or war damage), and a few steam 'extras' to various Southern-served race courses ran into the 1950s and beyond, notably including the Royal Train to Tattenham Corner."

From Jeremy Clarke, "Hi Kevin, shows how slowly I read that I've only now got around to going through this volume! May I reiterate a correction I made earlier regarding the 4-COR/4-BUF/4-RES sets? On page 57 Alan Blackburn states the motor coaches of these units had two 275hp motors. They were, in fact, the same as those provided for the 6-PUL/6-PAN sets for the Brighton line, of 225hp only. It is believed Maunsell would have preferred to put four motored bogies under the Portsmouth schemes' sets as well but Mr Walker would not agree with the expenditure. I agree the CORs could run very fast downhill but from personal experience over several years, they always appeared to labour on the steeper uphill sections of the 'Direct', Portsmouth, Witley to Haslemere for example and particularly off the coastal plain from Havant to Buriton tunnel. (There was a 45mph limit imposed due to curvature for about one mile south of Buriton tunnel - Ed.)

"The Mid-Sussex north of Horsham presented different if no less difficult problems. The sharp climb to Sutton after the heavily speed-restricted passing of Mitcham Junction for example, as well as the broken climb through the Mole Valley from the permanent restriction over the curves between Dorking North and Betchworth tunnel, to Holmwood. Similarly the 4½ miles northbound out of the Low Weald to Ockley was particularly sharp.

"The 6-PUL/6-PAN sets really could run, though the riding of the motor coaches was often dreadfully rough, not the vehicle in which to take a hot drink to the lips! The 4-COR sets and their ilk certainly rode better though they could be very lively at speed. A driver hoping to make up time could provide his passengers with a very uncomfortable few minutes on the descent from Haslemere to Godalming, though the speed restrictions south of Buriton and through Rowlands Castle could rather temper those hopes Portsmouth-bound."

From Jon Cooter, "Hello Kevin, alas, me again! (Jon - not at all, your comments are always welcome - Ed.) I still thoroughly enjoy SW and despite being born in the first half of the previous century when steam was king (and with hindsight held my railway interest above other facets of the industry). I am gradually getting to grips with jargon and abbreviations. You've probably guessed there's a "but" coming …..Here it is - SW20:p79   para 3

28 December 1951. 'British Railways, Southern Region has inaugurated a mobile school for motor drivers. Travelling around the Southern area, the school in a railway coach is fitted with part of a motor chassis and steering gear and lessons are given with the aid of model streets and traffic. Seen are Driver E Pilat (left) being instructed by Inspector A G West, while Inspector J Hamblett (right) teaches Driver E G Beaumont about the steering.'

down "Taking CIG/BIG stock …. have you ever had to manually apply or take off the electric parking brake in the mark 1 series? If you have, you'd fully applaud that the later builds reverted to traditional hand brakes and why they never ran on the south western side.

How could you as editor allow such an opaque uninformative and perhaps arrogant, elitist statement? How many of your readers do you think ever had opportunity to apply such a brake (or take it off)? What is the chap talking about? Was it complicated/difficult/unreliable? "South Western side" of what? BR(S)? old LSWR? where ever the place/area being referred to the readers who have not applied/removed such a brake have no idea what the guy is on about.

"I can concoct similar turgid text from my own sphere of work/interest: If I wrote to you saying "This weekend collected three Leiodes cinnamomea in my FIT, so you know what that means" you'd probably, like me, be getting the green ink bottle open. (explanation = on Sunday I found three beetles, species Leiodes cinnamomea, in a flight interception trap so this indicates truffle fungi grow in this woodland). This would be crystal clear to anyone with a knowledge of British beetles, just as the brake matter would be to anyone who has ever driven CIG/BIG stock - but in each case a very small minority will have this specialist knowledge. (Point taken - Ed.)

"SW is there to inform, amongst other things, so please if a contributor submits a similar text, meaningless to all but a privileged few, please, please knock it back and ask the author to enlighten us. I for one would very much like to know what it is about this type of brake and where it was never used and indeed how it was activated etc etc. There's doubtless an interesting few para's here masquerading as inaccessible jargon.

Right - *Steel indicator shelter on an almost new No 850, awaiting departure from Waterloo.*

Bottom - *Progress in the construction of the new Southampton Central station in July 1935. Eighty years later and we may see yet further similar development if the latest plans for rebuilding at this location proceed. Amongst other changes suggested for the South West trains area, two new platforms and a new freight line are proposed at Southampton. For the full report see: http:// www.networkrail.co.uk/long-term-planning-process/wessex-route-study/ (Notice also the destination board on the side of the coach….more on these and carriage roof boards in general in Issue No 31 for July.)*

I feel better now! Time to dissect the male cinnamomea and make its aedeagus up as a clove oil mount (oops! sorry). Keep up the good work."

Now from Jim Smallbone, "Kevin, the two photographs at Petersfield's Midhurst platform (SW28) has a Mr Percy Berriman and not Mr Bill Tupper as the station foreman overseeing the departure of the train. A photograph of Mr Bill Tupper appears in the Middleton Press publication Branch Lines Around Midhurst."

Next from Nicholas Owen, "A quick response to discussion about the two Southern Double Decker units. I was very fortunate to get cab rides for trips scheduled one weekday evening for Nos. 4001 and 4002. It would have been about 1969. The first run from from Slade Green was ECS to Charing Cross, then a service train to Dartford in the "shoulder" of the rush hour...i.e. about 4 pm, thus avoiding too much of a crush for passengers. Returning from Dartford, the second trip out of "the Cross" was just after the main peak hour traffic, for the same reason. The driving cab equipment, incidentally, was a SUB "three a clock to nine o'clock" controller with an EPB-style self lapping EP and Westinghouse brake. *(Note to Editor: I was glad to contribute a thought to issue 28, though perturbed at first garbled sentence...do hope I didn't send it over that way! Well done, though...another great issue)*

And finally a few lovely memories from Chris Sayers-Leavy, "When I arrived at the small loco hauled C&W depot at Clapham Junc. in 1972, I found a depot in decline, its work had been seriously curtailed after the Bournemouth electrification and it was reduced to working on 'vans' and whatever else it could get, such as the re-flooring of 'carflats' of all things...... The shed was run on very traditional lines and whilst you had to provide your own basic tools, specialist tools were kept under lock and key by the chargehand. One day whilst doing a job, I needed to clean up a damaged thread on a bolt that had been removed from some item of equipment – and as there were no new replacement bolts of the right size available – I asked if there was a 'die' available to do the job.

"I was told that there was and I was taken upstairs

to the chargehands little office and to a steel cupboard that was unlocked and a large flat wooden box was brought out and placed on the table – inside was a complete set of Whitworth taps, dies and the necessary wrenches – all pristine looking – and each item was stamped LB&SCR !!!!!!!

"Now, considering that the 'Brighton' had merged into the SR in 1923 and the LB&SCR marking was an earlier form of what latterly was shortened to just LBSC – these items must have dated from the early 1900s and were thus about 60 years old !!! I duly signed for the one that I needed and whilst descending the stairs back to the workshop – I wondered how they had survived in such a good condition over all those years........Still pondering the age of the die, I set about using it, only to find out immediately how they had survived so long – as it was very blunt ! It turned out that the entire contents of the box were all the same – well worn out !!!!!

"As a technical aside, the taps & dies would have been made of what is known as 'Carbon steel' and they would have needed periodic re-sharpening (a specialist job), whereas more modern items are made of HSS steel with a cutting edge that lasts a lot longer.

"I left the depot before it finally closed (as I was one of the 'last in' I did not want to be one of the 'first out' !) and I have often wondered if anybody saved the box of taps & dies ???? or whether like so much of this sort of equipment – it was just scrapped...........Many years later whilst working for NWR I had to revisit an office at Clapham Junc. in the yard there and I could find no trace of the original depot whatsoever, but the track layout was the same and you could still see the area where the depot once stood........"

(Anyone interested in my particular favourite topic, 'Leader' of course, may be interested to learn that Simon Lilley has advised of a page that appears on 'flicker' one of which images depicts the Brighton Works shunter moving 'Leader' bogies in the area of the works. https://www.flickr.com/photos/davidwf2009/sets/72157626573634846/)

Left - *Crawley good yard with private owner wagons from 'M Nightingale'.*

Right - *Shefflex railcar at Selsey, c1930. Terry Cole collection.*

With a connection to both the 4-COR article that appears earlier in this issue, and also Havant station, junction for the Hayling line described opposite, a scene at Aldershot with a brand new Portsmouth line set alongside an M7 in July 1937.

AVE ATQUE VALE *........
HAYLING FAREWELL

Jeffery Grayer recalls the last weekend of the Hayling Island branch which closed to all traffic over half a century ago in November 1963.

S aturday 2nd November 1963 was the final day of timetabled services on the 4 mile 52 chain branch line from the junction at Havant to the terminus at Hayling Island. It was perhaps not surprising, against the background of the Beeching Report that was published in the spring of 1963, that this line should have been slated for closure. However, the line was not included in the Beeching cuts as it had already been selected for closure the previous year. Its selection was not due to operating economics, indeed quite the reverse for its summer holiday traffic plus a regular if smaller commuter trade saw it returning small operating profits at the beginning of the 1960s; in 1961 an operating profit of £2,000 was recorded. Whilst income was naturally of a seasonal nature, BR's monthly statistics for tickets collected being 2,077 in March 1961 but rocketing to 32,176 in August 1961, the line's annual income more than matched its operating costs. Its candidacy for closure ultimately stemmed from the need to replace the 1000 foot long timber viaduct at Langston at a reported cost of £400,000 – clearly an unacceptable sum for such a marginal line to justify.

On 12th December 1962 a packed meeting of the local Transport Users Consultative Committee was convened at Havant Town Hall attended by local people and more than 50 organisations such as Hayling Island Chamber of Trade, Hayling Island Residents' Association, the Havant and Bedhampton Electors and Ratepayers Association, the Portsmouth Trades Council, and the Urban District Council of Havant and Waterlooville. This volume of protests was overruled with the

Above - A little girl, who must now be in her 50s, admires the diminutive lines of Stroudley Terrier No. 32650 waiting in the bay platform at Havant, with safety valves lifting, on the morning of 2 November 1963, the final weekend of branch services.

Left - No. 32650 takes water in the bay platform at Havant against a background of cars of the period. Oddly enough, watering was undertaken here but coaling was done at Hayling terminus.

*** AVE ATQUE VALE - "HAIL AND FAREWELL"**

opposing arguments for the cost of repairs to Langston Harbour bridge and of replacing the supposedly "ageing coaching stock" winning the day and the decision was made to recommend to the Minister of Transport that the railway should be closed. This "ageing coaching stock" proved to be something of a red herring as much of it consisted of 1956 built Mk Is which were, in August 1963, supplemented with S1000S the glass fibre bodied coach, all of which were subsequently put to use elsewhere on the Southern Region! This unusual glass fibre-bodied coach was out-shopped from Eastleigh on the 7 March 1963 as DS70200 and was sent to Brighton to operate in the "Lancing Belle", the staff train for Lancing Carriage Works. Sometime shortly before 4th August 1963 it was re-numbered S1000S and sent to operate on the Hayling Island service. It was around this time that the project to build complete vehicles in GRP was cancelled. It is believed that the cost of manufacture was considered too high to put such a vehicle into production. When the Hayling Island branch closed, S1000S operated for a short time on the West London Line service between Clapham Junction and Kensington Olympia before it was transferred back into the "Lancing Belle" formation. The "Lancing Belle" last operated as a specific service on 3/7/64 after which it went back again to the West London service where it stayed until the end of steam working in July 1967. After this the vehicle was sent to Micheldever for storage until finally withdrawn in January 1973. It was quickly sold to the East Somerset Railway at Cranmore on 14/2/73, where it can be seen today. Only Maunsell corridor compo coaches 6697/6699 of 1935 vintage were in fact scrapped as a result of the closure, the other coaches continuing to work elsewhere on the region; so the excuse of "ageing coaching stock" was in the event hardly valid.

The Minister of Transport approved closure of the Hayling branch line subject to the following conditions –

Additional Southdown bus services must be arranged beforehand.

A luggage in advance service must continue between Havant and Hayling

The first 6 months of closure were to be regarded as a trial period during which the suitability of the bus service should be reviewed – interestingly this did not extend long enough to include the summer months of 1964 the time when the ability of buses to cope with holiday crowds was really put to the test.

BR must keep themselves informed, and inform the MoT, of any changes to the substitute bus services.

Closure followed after a delay in organising the replacement bus services with the last public train running on 2 November 1963. The final train, the "Hayling Railway Farewell Tour", ran the following day behind the oldest working locomotive then operating on British Railways – No. 32636 built in 1872.

By the early 1960s the condition of Langston bridge, by then 95 years old, was giving cause for concern. This unfortunately came at a time when increasing attention was being paid to railway economics particularly on branch and secondary routes. "Modern Railways" magazine for September 1962 under the banner headline "No Trains To Hayling Island ?" reported the plans for closure. Another factor of course was the age of the Terriers and the difficulty of finding replacement motive power. Had the will and the finances been there for capital investment, lightweight diesel railcars would have been one answer but given the state of the bridge it is unlikely whether even the introduction of these units would have saved the day.

The final Saturday came round all too quickly and No. 32650 worked in the morning with a three coach rake,

With a feather of steam from the safety valves No. 32670 barks round the curve in true Terrier fashion having just left Havant with another trip to Hayling.

which included the glass fibre coach, joined by fellow Terriers Nos. 32662 and 32670 in the afternoon with another three coach set. A wreath was carried on the smokebox door of No. 32662, although the locomotive itself was rather scruffy in appearance. A glorious sunset enhanced the last evening and many passengers took the opportunity for a last ride and to snap up tickets, handbills, luggage labels and other souvenirs. For the last return journey the two 3-coach sets were coupled together and the rare sight of a six coach formation left Havant to the traditional accompaniment of exploding detonators, with No. 32662 leading and No. 32650 at the rear end. The night was brightly moonlit and, despite the cold, many of the intermediate vantage points were packed with spectators with crowds on both the diminutive Langston and North Hayling platforms. After a brief turnround of just 5 minutes, so typical of the tightly-timed services on this branch, No. 32650 led off from Hayling with the final timetabled service. The local newspaper recorded the event thus –

"Passengers joined hands and sang Auld Lang Syne in the guard's van of the last "Hayling Billy" on Saturday night as it steamed, with whistle sounding continuously, round the last bend to Havant station...people thronged fences and gates and other vantage points. Curtains were drawn back, windows thrown open, and even tape recorders were produced to catch the last familiar and very distinctive sounds. No doubt there wasn't a dry eye in the house as the faithful old servants panted and puffed their way into the platform at Havant."

As the train eased round the sharp radius curve into Havant, again with exploding detonators as a backdrop, with the last up service train, the Havant Station Master was waiting on the platform, illuminated as it was by numerous flashbulbs as cameras recorded the scene.

The following day, Sunday when there was no normal winter service, a five coach special, made up of four BR compartment seconds and a Maunsell brake-composite and conveying over 450 passengers, traversed the line with Nos. 32636 and 32670, one at each end facing outwards for the benefit of photographers. After a nine minute late start from Havant, photographic stops were made at both Langston, for some eight minutes, and North Hayling, for 13 minutes, the longer stop here no doubt being due to the short platform requiring the train to draw up. A one-minute early arrival was achieved at Hayling at 14:34 where spectators were numbered in the hundreds. Promptly at 14:50, following the waving of the green flag and blowing of the whistle by Guard Fred Morris, No. 32670 led the final departure from Hayling, once more to the sound of exploding detonators, with its crossing of the bridge for the final time, augmented by the hooting of a steam launch

No. 32646 rattles along south of Havant with its three coach load. After a spell on the Meon Valley line, this locomotive was placed outside the Hayling Billy public house on the island in its guise of No. 46 "Newington" before finding a home on the Isle of Wight Steam railway

No. 32640 simmers at journey's end at Hayling on 8ᵗʰ August 1959 – hard to believe that just 4 years later the line would be approaching its finale. This locomotive was withdrawn in September 1963, just failing to be included in the "Final Quintet" of 'Terriers' which were operational at closure of the line two months later. Purchased by Butlins she was displayed at their Pwllheli camp from 1964 - 1973 before moving to the Isle of Wight Steam Railway, where she can be seen in the guise of No. W11 "Newport".

moored adjacent to the Langston Sailing Club HQ. The special took just over ten minutes to complete this last journey. Upon departure from Havant the Terriers headed for their base at Fratton shed and subsequent withdrawal. The whole day was made more memorable by a burst of brilliant winter sunshine which enhanced the spectacle for both photographers and linesiders alike. By the last day there were just five Terriers left in BR service and they were all withdrawn following closure of the line. Remarkably, no fewer than 9 examples have been preserved plus an original

Stroudley A1 now housed at the National Railway Museum.

After closure of the line a Terrier, No. 32646, did return to Hayling in 1966, but only as a static exhibit outside a public house, the appropriately named "Hayling Billy". It was transferred to the Isle of Wight Steam Railway in 1979 where it can still be seen. Hopes were high that a preservation society could re-open the line and an ex-Blackpool tramcar, No. 11 of 1935 vintage, arrived at Havant goods yard in September 1965. However, in 1966 the track was taken up, the opening span of the bridge was removed and by January 1969 the tramcar had gone. Incredibly, over half a century has now passed since the last diminutive Stroudley 'Terrier' puffed its way across Langston Bridge, the structure, which ultimately proved to be the Achilles' heel of the line, bringing to an end its operation under BR and effectively quashing any realistic hopes of a life in preservation.

From May 1966, No. 32646 did duty outside the "Hayling Billy" public house owned by Brickwoods Brewery who returned it to Stroudley livery as No.46 "Newington". Brickwoods' successor – Whitbread Wessex – donated the deteriorating engine to the Isle of Wight Steam Railway.

The former Hayling Billy No. 32646 seen as No. W8 "Freshwater" at Havenstreet. Having arrived on the Isle of Wight in June 1979, she returned to steam on 21 June 1981 after a rapid overhaul. No. W8 has been a stalwart member of the locomotive fleet, a brand new boiler being commissioned in 1998 at a cost of £35,000 from Israel Newton of Bradford.

Across the bleak mudflats of Langston Harbour the decaying railway viaduct awaits its fate.

Top - *View of the moribund viaduct looking south in the mid-1960s. The pylons carried the island's electricity supply.*

Centre - *The timber trestle construction of the viaduct is evident in this late 1960s view.*

Bottom - *A derelict Hayling terminus awaits demolition. The Gothic-style building was designed by F Whitaker incorporating timber framing with inset red and white herring-bone brickwork. The canopy was saved and re-erected at the Hollycombe Steam collection near Liphook.*

Opposite top - *Piles of earth lie on the former permanent way, the goods shed being the only former railway building still standing at Hayling today. It is now the theatre of the Hayling Amateur Dramatic Society.*

Opposite bottom - *What the Hayling line was all about – a packed train of returning holidaymakers rounds the curve into Havant with No. 32646 running bunker first on 25 June 1961.*

Table 51 — HAVANT and HAYLING ISLAND

Miles	Down	Week Days until 30th May, Mondays to Fridays from 1st June, 1964
		am am am am am am am am ... ... pm pm pm SO SO pm pm pm ... SX SO SX SO SX SO
—	Havant .. .. dep	6 30 7 34 8 15 9 14 10 19 11 35 ... 12 35 1 35 2 20 3 35 4 46 5 33 ... 6 20 6 34 7 20 7 34 8 20 8 38 ...
1	Langston	6 34 7 37 8 18 9 17 10 8 11 38 ... 12 38 1 38 2 23 3 38 4 49 5 36 ... 6 23 6 37 7 23 7 37 8 23 8 41 ...
2¾	North Hayling	7 41 8 22 9 22 10 26 11 42 ... 12 42 1 42 2 27 3 42 4 53 5 40 ... 6 27 6 41 7 27 7 41 8 27 8 45 ..
4½	Hayling Island .... arr	6 43 7 47 8 28 9 28 10 32 11 48 ... 12 48 1 48 2 33 3 48 4 59 5 46 ... 6 33 6 47 7 33 7 47 8 33 8 51 ..

Down	Saturdays—Commencing 6th June, 1964
	am am am am am am am am am am am pm pm pm pm pm pm pm pm pm pm pm pm pm pm pm pm pm pm
Havant .. .. dep	6 30 7 34 8 15 9 14 10 5 10 35 11 5 11 35 12 5 12 35 1 5 1 35 2 5 2 35 3 5 3 35 4 5 4 35 5 5 5 35 6 5 6 35 7 35 8 38
Langston	6 34 7 37 8 18 9 17 10 8 ... 11 8 ... 12 8 ... 1 8 ... 2 8 ... 3 8 ... 4 8 ... 5 8 ... 6 8 6 38 7 38 8 41
North Hayling	7 41 8 22 9 24 10 12 ... 11 12 ... 12 12 ... 1 12 ... 2 12 ... 3 12 ... 4 12 ... 5 12 ... 6 12 6 42 7 42 8 45
Hayling Island .... arr	6 43 7 47 8 28 9 30 10 18 10 45 11 18 11 45 12 18 12 45 1 18 1 45 2 18 2 45 3 18 3 45 4 18 4 45 5 18 5 45 6 18 6 48 7 48 8 51

Down	Sundays—Commencing 12th April, 1964
	am am pm pm pm pm pm pm pm pm
Havant .. .. dep	10 35 ... 11 35 ... 12 35 ... 1 35 ... 2 35 ... 3 35 ... 5 35 ... 6 35 ... 7 35 ...
Langston	10 38 ... 11 38 ... 12 38 ... 1 38 ... 2 38 ... 3 38 ... 5 38 ... 6 38 ... 7 38 ...
North Hayling	10 42 ... 11 42 ... 12 42 ... 1 42 ... 2 42 ... 3 42 ... 5 42 ... 6 42 ... 7 42 ...
Hayling Island .... arr	10 48 ... 11 48 ... 12 48 ... 1 48 ... 2 48 ... 3 48 ... 5 48 ... 6 48 ... 7 48 ...

Miles	Up	Week Days until 30th May, Mondays to Fridays from 1st June, 1964
		am am am am am am pm SO SO SX pm pm pm SX SO pm pm
—	Hayling Island .. dep	7 2 7 55 8 35 9 45 10 52 11 55 ... 12 55 1 20 1 47 2 58 ... 4 16 5 6 5 57 6 50 ... 6 52 7 52 8 56 ...
2	North Hayling	7 6 7 59 8 39 9 49 10 56 11 59 ... 12 59 1 59 3 13 4 ... 4 20 5 10 6 1 6 54 ... 6 56 7 56 9 0 ...
3½	Langston	7 11 8 4 8 44 9 54 11 1 12 4 ... 1 4 2 55 15 6 6 59 ... 7 1 8 1 9 5 ...
4½	Havant .. .. arr	7 15 8 8 8 48 9 58 11 5 12 8 ... 1 8 2 8 3 10 3 15 ... 4 29 5 19 6 10 7 3 ... 7 5 8 5 9 9 ...

Up	Saturdays—Commencing 6th June, 1964
	am am am am am am am am pm pm pm pm pm pm pm pm pm pm pm pm pm pm pm pm pm pm
Hayling Island .. dep	7 2 7 55 8 35 9 45 10 20 10 47 11 20 11 47 12 20 12 47 1 20 1 47 2 20 2 47 3 20 3 47 4 20 4 47 5 20 5 47 6 20 6 49 7 17 7 53 8 56
North Hayling	7 6 7 59 8 39 9 49 ... 10 51 ... 11 51 ... 12 51 ... 1 51 ... 2 51 ... 3 51 ... 4 51 ... 5 51 ... 6 53 7 21 7 57 9 0
Langston	7 11 8 4 8 44 9 54 ... 10 56 ... 11 56 ... 12 56 ... 1 56 ... 2 56 ... 3 56 ... 4 56 ... 5 56 ... 6 58 7 26 8 2 9 5
Havant .. .. arr	7 15 8 8 8 48 9 58 10 30 11 0 11 30 12 0 12 30 1 0 1 30 2 0 2 30 3 0 3 30 4 0 4 30 5 0 5 30 6 0 6 30 7 2 7 30 8 6 9 9

Up	Sundays—Commencing 12th April, 1964
	am am pm pm pm pm pm pm pm
Hayling Island .. dep	10 55 ... 11 55 ... 12 55 ... 1 55 ... 2 55 ... 4 55 ... 5 55 ... 6 55 ... 7 55 ...
North Hayling	10 59 ... 11 59 ... 12 59 ... 1 59 ... 2 59 ... 4 59 ... 5 59 ... 6 59 ... 7 59 ...
Langston	11 4 ... 12 4 ... 1 4 ... 2 4 ... 3 4 ... 5 4 ... 6 4 ... 7 4 ... 8 4 ...
Havant .. .. arr	11 8 ... 12 8 ... 1 8 ... 2 8 ... 3 8 ... 5 8 ... 6 8 ... 7 8 ... 8 8 ...

SO Saturdays only.   **SX** Mondays to Fridays.

Final Summer Timetable, the Saturday service of which was operated on the final afternoon of timetabled services in November 1963.

From the July 1963, 'Modern Railways'.

HAYLING LIGHT RAILWAY SOCIETY

"The Hayling Light Railway Society has been formed with the object of acquiring the Havant - Hayling Island branch line from British Railways, who plan to close the branch completely to all traffic. The Society proposes to operate the branch line as a light railway using electric railcars, three of which may be ex-Eastern Region cars from the Grimsby and Immingham Electric Light Railway, now closed. The Society is also interested in the preservation of an A1X 'Terrier', also some suitable coaching stock. Platignum ball-pens stamped 'Hayling Light Railway Society' are being sold (1s 5d post free, from R S Cromwell, Wishford, The Marld, Ashtead, Surrey) in aid of the 'Terrier' fund. Membership particulars may be obtained from the Society's Hon. Secretary, N G Sloman, 1 Beaufort Avenue, Fareham, Hants. A meeting at which the Society's proposals will be outlined fully will be held on July 13, at the British Legion Hall, Gable Head, Hayling Island, commencing at 2 30 p.m. Any person interested is invited to attend."

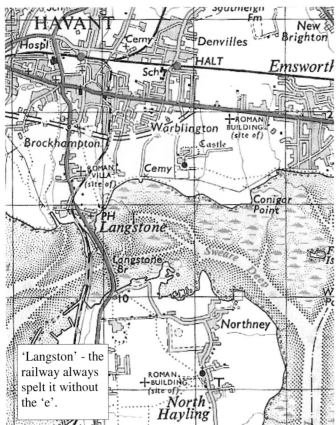

Langston Bridge – ultimate cause of the line's demise. Map reproduced with the kind permission of the Ordnance Survey.

'Langston' - the railway always spelt it without the 'e'.

Appendix 'A': Hayling Farewell Railtour

Organised by the Locomotive Club of Great Britain 3-11-63

30512	Waterloo - Alton - Eastleigh - Fratton
34088/31791	Fratton - Portsmouth Dockyard
31791	Portsmouth Dockyard - Havant
32636/32670	Havant - Hayling - Havant
30531/30543	Havant - Chichester - Lavant - Chichester - Horsham - Three Bridges - Victoria

	Schedule	Actual
Havant	11.58a - 13.50d	13.50 - 13.59
Langston	13.54a - 14.10d	14.02 - 14.10½
North Hayling	14.15a - 14.30d	14.15 - 14.28½
Hayling Island	14.35a - 14.50d	14.34 - 14.50
Havant	15.00a - 15.15d	15.00½ -15.18½

Appendix 'B': Terriers associated with the Hayling Line 1960 - 63

Number	Withdrawn	Preservation
32636	11/63	
32640+	9/63	Isle of Wight
32646+	11/63	Isle of Wight
32650+	11/63	Spa Valley
32655+	5/60	Bluebell
32661	4/63	
32662+	11/63	Bressingham
32670+	11/63	K&ESR
32678+	10/63	K&ESR

+ Preserved. In addition three further Terriers are preserved – Nos. 32654 (Canada) 32672 (Bluebell Railway) and 32682 (NRM – A1 Class)

During its stay on the nearby West Somerset Railway, which lasted from 1975-83, No. 32678 is seen undergoing some cosmetic restoration in the yard at Minehead (above) and (below) adjacent to the main platform. It moved to Woolwich and subsequently to the K&ESR where restoration was completed in 1909. It paid a return visit to the WSR in 2004.

Billy Butlin added to the attractions at his Minehead Camp when in 1964 he brought 6229 "Duchess of Hamilton" and LBSCR 'Terrier' "Knowle" to the site. They left the camp in 1975 and No. 6229 has subsequently been returned to streamlined condition and is displayed at the NRM whilst "Knowle" or No. 32678 is currently based on the K&ESR.

ALICE TUBBS OF DURLEY
Roger Simmonds

When one thinks of remote railway locations it is easy to think of the Highlands of Scotland or a remote spot in mid-Wales, however even in central Hampshire it was possible. Durley Halt was located on the LSWR branch from Botley to Bishops Waltham, it even won a competition in a magazine once, voted as the station one was the most unlikely to alight at.

The line opened in 1863 very much a local affair promoted by the Bishops Waltham Railway Company and operated by the LSWR, who took over the impoverished affair in 1881 following years of receivership. A level crossing existed at Durley from the railway's earliest days serving a minor road to Durley Mill and a handful of small dwellings. A house for the crossing keeper was provided in 1881. The first occupants are not known, but eventually the Elliott family lived there as confirmed by the 1901 census. Harry Elliott had earlier worked on the permanent way, possibly as lengthman or indeed the ganger. As a young man it is believed he may have even been involved in the construction of the line in the 1860's. Later no doubt because of age or physical limits, he became crossing keeper at Durley and moved into the cottage. Harry and his wife Isabella had two children, Alice and Walter, both destined to be employed by the LSWR and later the SR.

Eventually when Alice was 17 years of age in 1907, she was taken on as the crossing keeper after her father Harry retired. Her main duty of course was the opening and closing of the crossing gates, ensuring safe passage of trains and safety of road users. The latter would mainly be of carts transporting materials to and from the mill. Alice was notified of approaching trains by a bell ringing in the cottage, this was rung by the signalmen at Bishops Waltham and Botley respectively.

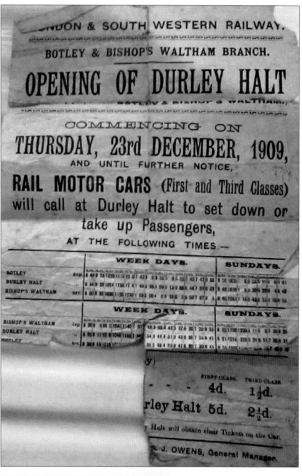

Alice Tubbs seen on the platform at Durley Halt in 1930. Courtesy Ann Piper,

ALICE TUBBS OF DURLEY

After two years in this role Alice was notified that the LSWR had agreed to a request petition for a Halt to be provided for Durley residents. This was approved and made public in December 1909 evidenced by a surviving notice. A local Botley based carpenter Charlie Tubbs was contracted to build the Halt which was to be located hard by the crossing. After a short while it was clear Charlie and Alice had taken a shine to each other and they were eventually married. They lived in the railway cottage along with Alice's brother Walter who by now was a member of the local permanent way gang. Fortunately a surviving family photograph was taken of Alice Tubbs on the platform in 1930 and is reproduced here. It is only the second known image of the Halt ever to be found (the other one appeared in *"The Bishops Waltham Railway"*, a book by the author published by Wild Swan).

Alice's father Harry came out to give the "all clear" to the first train to stop and leave Durley Halt on the 23 December 1909. Encouragingly what had been a simple platform, three lamps and a station name board plus a shelter were provided in November 1910 at an estimated cost of £35. It is not known if Charlie Tubbs built this too, but quite likely. Sadly the Halt was destined to close when the passenger service ceased at the end of 1932. Fittingly Alice (along with her daughter) were the last passengers to board a train from Durley Halt to Botley on the final service on 31 December 1932.

Alice remained as crossing keeper for 47 years retiring in 1954, an event which attracted the attention of the *Southern Daily Echo* who included a photograph of Alice and her brother waving to the engine crew of a passing goods train. In reality though this was somewhat staged as Alice had retired some time before the photograph was taken and had moved out of the railway house (by now rather derelict) to a cottage further up the lane - journalistic license perhaps!. Alice was not replaced and the crossing became unmanned now, operated by train crews, until the line finally closed in April 1962.

The railway connection carried on in the family with two of Alice's three children. Daughter Winifred (or Winnie as she was known) became a Porter at Botley station and eventually married Arthur Smith, who was the Station Master at Botley at the time. This is believed to be during the 1940's when many men had signed up for the war effort. Alice's son Lionel became a signalman and eventually was put in charge of Portchester station. Lionel (who by now had married Doris) then moved to Kings Worthy (presumably just after the DN&S line transferred to the Southern Region in 1950). As there was no station house available, the couple were accommodated in one of the railway cottages at Winchester Junction. Lionel was quite active in the community at Kings Worthy and a memorial to him still exists by way of the village hall being named after him.

Acknowledgements
Sally Piper (Alice Tubbs granddaughter)
Ann Piper

Durley Halt with Winifred Tubbs (Alice's daughter).

Durley Crossing cottage.

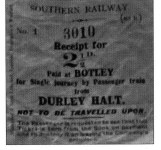

Top - *Durley crossing keeper's cottage,*
Below left (2) - *Alice by the crossing, the approaching train is heading south towards Botley.*

Above - *Porchester , with Lionel Tubbs and Winifred.*

A LITTLE LOCAL DIFFICULTY!

A disagreement between the SR and GWR over coach parking at Exmouth Station
Recounted by Terry Cole.

Pad.256.

28th May, 1929.

Dear Milne,

Great Western Railway Road Services.

Further to my letter of the 9th May, I have received a letter dated 25th idem from one of our people, of which the following is an extract:-

"...Our Exmouth Agent reports to me that two G.W.Company's "road motors were at Exmouth yesterday (20th May) with "passengers from Plymouth, and that the Drivers asked "permission to berth the vehicles in our yard, which was "declined.
" Kindly note."

I must admit at once that I admire your Driver intensely - for pure cheek he has got the whole continent of America beaten; but apart from that the whole matter is not so pleasant, and your folk do not seem to have put into effect Minute No.3851 of the General Managers' Conference, or indeed any other means of asking "by your leave", and I am afraid if things go on like this there will be a volcanic eruption one of these days - and volcanic lava is hot!

Even the G.W/L.& S.W.Agreement of May, 1910, in the penultimate paragraph of Clause 2, legislated for this sort of thing, but has rather been treated with contempt in our various 'bus negotiations, but I suggest that enthusiasum has overstepped the bounds of decency, and the time has come when we must ask you to curb this enthusiasum.

Will you look into the matter, and let me hear from you, for Sir Herbert - when he knows of it - is sure to want to know, not only how much we are going to get out of this specific case, but what is being done to safeguard against its recurrence.

Yours sincerely,

J. Milne, Esq.,
Assistant General Manager,
Great Western Railway.

These skirmishes between the SR and GWR had obviously been going on for some time and we pick up the story on Monday 29 May 1929 when two coach drivers from the Great Western had the temerity to ask permission to berth their vehicles in the yard of the Southern station at Exmouth. Fair enough you might think, no big deal here. But no, it produced the following personal letter on Tuesday 28 May from Major Szlumper in the Southern Railway General Manager's office to J Milne, Assistant General Manager of the Great Western Railway.

Major Szlumper, assured of having the moral high ground, writes as follows:,

"Dear Milne…..

The letter is confident, cocky even, and almost

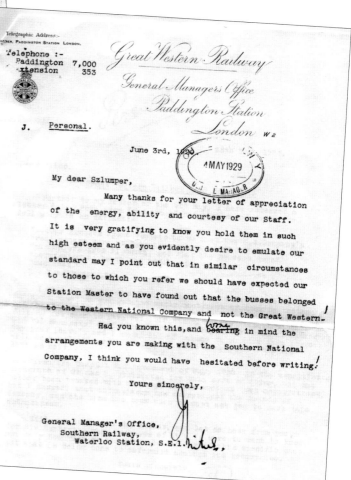

'schoolboy like', in its tone, especially in the threat to tell 'Teacher' in the person of Sir Herbert Walker!

Mr Milne checks his facts and on Monday 3 June replies thus:

"My dear Szlumper……

Game, Set and Match, Milne, I think!

Oh dear, poor old Szlumper. This was obviously not the reply he expected. He really has got egg on his face. Let's hope he didn't tell 'Sir Herbert' otherwise he would certainly be standing in the naughty corner with the 'Dunce's cap' on.

Top - *S&DJR 2-8-0 7F No. 53810 stands outside Bath Green Park engine shed as it has its smoke-box door attended to on 11 April 1963.*

Left - *Ex-LMS 2P 4-4-0 No. 40700 pilots an un-identified BR Standard Class 5 as together they haul a heavy train up the 1 in 50 gradient south from Radstock on 2 August 1958. Note the Whitaker tablet exchange apparatus attached to the side of the 2P's tender indicating that it is on home ground and available to exchange tokens on the single line sections further south. The first two coaches are LMS Period 2 stock. (All images by the author.)*

SOMERSET & DORSET JOINT
Part 1: Radstock to Shepton Mallet
Peter Tatlow

My colleague in the New Works Drawing Office at Waterloo, David Andrews, had encouraged me to obtain a line-side walking pass, and I looked forward to making the most of the 1958 August Bank Holiday weekend. Despite his expressed desire to photograph Great Western engines, having recently read about the Somerset and Dorset, I persuaded him that better views of steam locomotives hard at work were to be obtained on the steep grades either side of Masbury Summit, as the line made its way south from Bath with heavy trains of holiday makers heading for Bournemouth and other south coast resorts. As in those early days my pass was limited to only a few lengths of line, we popped downstairs to the Publicity & Public Relations Office, where the friendly old boy who dealt with such matters was happy to add the S&D lines and wished us an enjoyable trip.

At that time, railway office staff were given the Friday afternoon before a Bank Holiday off, and in deference to my friend's sensibilities, we headed to Paddington to catch the 1.15pm to Bath Spa. The next morning, however, found us on the 8.15am from Bath Green Park station for the first leg of the day to Radstock North. From here we walked along the railway the eleven miles to Shepton Mallet, photographing all the trains as they passed. The double-line climbs steadily from Radstock for seven and a half miles into the Mendip Hills, mainly at 1 in 50/60, to the summit at Masbury, 811 feet above sea level, before falling at similar grades, apart from a brief respite at Shepton Mallet, all the way to Evercreech Junction.

Originally conceived as a line of 65 miles linking Burnham, on the Bristol Channel, with shipping to South Wales, to Poole on the south coast and before Bournemouth had been developed, this failed to produce the traffic hoped for. The construction of a 25-mile-long line northwards to Bath was then undertaken, there to meet up with the Midland Railway with connections to Bristol, Gloucester and on to the Midlands. With the company by then financially exhausted, the LSWR and MR seeing the potential traffic from the south coast to the Midlands, avoiding the then-still-broad gauge GW, stepped in and leased the S&D from 1875. In 1923, this was converted into joint ownership. Closure of the system, apart from a

On its own, another BR Standard Class 5 on the same day drifts downhill with a north-bound train between Midsomer Norton and Radstock. It carries express headlamps, while the reporting number '993' chalked on the plate below the smoke-box, the prefix letter being indecipherable.

An LMS 4F 0-6-0 precedes an unidentified LMS 4-6-0 Black Five through a shallow rock cutting south of the short twin-bore Chilcompton Tunnel, actually a heavily skewed road crossing.

few short lengths for freight traffic only, came about on 7 March 1966.

With the LSWR and later the SR taking on responsibility for the civil engineering aspects of the joint venture, the Midland/LMS assumed that for motive power. As a result in due course every day duties were undertaken by MR/LMS types, such as 4-4-0 2Ps, 0-6-0 3Fs and 4Fs, and Johnson 0-4-4Ts. There was also of course the 2-8-0 7Fs specially designed at Derby in 1914 for working freight on the steep gradients of the line. In the ordinary course of events this stock of locomotives was adequate to work the everyday traffic of the line.

With the coming of paid leave, holiday traffic had, however, already been building up prior to the outbreak of World War 2. Afterwards, straitened economic circumstances, as the country slowly recovered, with food rationing still in place, in the days before universal ownership of cars or cheap charter flight holidays on the Mediterranean, meant that most holidaymakers travelled by train to destinations in Great Britain. In addition, guest houses, if not hotels, partly due to rationing, tended to encourage bookings from Saturday to Saturday. On the S&DJ, as elsewhere, this led to the need for a considerable number of inter-regional special trains on summer Saturdays. From various points all over the Midlands and north of the country, many of these would require piloting over the Mendips. Motive power for these additional trains, apart from hijacking the 2-8-0s for passenger duties, was of course well beyond local resources, which would be fully occupied providing assistance banking the extra through trains and automatic single line token exchange facilities, as well as maintaining the basic local service. During our trip only two S&D 2-8-0s were seen, the first one, No. 53806 at Moorewood Sidings in consort with 4F No. 44211,

unfortunately catching us slightly by surprise with smoke drifting down to spoil the view.

As all trains had to reverse direction at Bath Green Park station, a change of engines was inevitable and the additional units would sometimes be loaned for the day from outside the S&D. At the time of our visit much of this was provided in the form of un-rebuilt West Country 4-6-2s, LMS and BR Standard 4-6-0s. All of this extraordinary activity was of course the quarry that the two of us sought to capture on film, as their engines struggled with heavy loads, hopefully displaying spectacular exhaust, if not pyrotechnics.

While passing through Chilcompton station, we were challenged by the signalman. On showing his walking permit for all non-electrified lines on the Southern Region, my friend was informed that the line north of Cole had been transferred to the Western Region on 2 April 1950! It was perhaps just as well then that mine specifically referred to the S&D, even if it had been issued at Waterloo. We continued the rest of our trip unmolested.

Upon reaching Shepton Mallet during the early afternoon, we took the local train to Evercreech Jct, from where we went onto Highbridge, changed to the GW main line again and down to Taunton. Here we spent the night, before continuing to a second steeply-graded line from Barnstaple to Ilfracombe. (See SW No 28.)

References
Dendy Marshall CF, *A history of the Southern Railway*, The Southern Railway, 1936, pp 132, 141, 161, 167, 174, 177, 229, 518.
Peters, I, *The Somerset & Dorset in modern times*, Trains Illustrated Summer Annual No. 3, p32.

No. 40563 of 1928 in combination with a 4-6-0 BR Standard 4 as they pass through Binegar on their way to the summit. This and other trains carry headlamps, indicating not an express freight or cattle train with continuous brake on less than one-third etc, as per general practice elsewhere, but the Southern Region code for a passenger train throughout between Bournemouth West and Bath Green Park

Two 0-6-0s head a south-bound train on the last stretch to the summit at Masbury with a long train of ex-LMS stock. Leading is No. 43216, an ex-S&DJR Johnson 3F, formerly No. 72. This is followed by a 4F.

Only two S&D 2-8-0s were seen during the trip, the first with smoke drifting down to spoil the view. The second seen here, was No. 53804 on its own approaching Winsor Tunnel from the south with a seven coach north-bound train. Note the tablet catcher extending from the side of the tender.

Another BR Standard Class 5 with express headlamps heading south between Winsor Hill and Shepton Mallet. The locomotive is displaying a train reporting number M976 indicating an inter-regional special originating on the Midland Division of the LMR. Note, however, the leading two coaches which were apparently part of a Gresley steel quintuple set.

Our walk along the line on 2 August 1958 from Radstock concluded on reaching Shepton Mallet, as 2P No. 40563 again pilots an unidentified un-rebuilt West Country with a south-bound train consisting of ex-LMS Period 3 stock in a mixture of both carmine and cream, and crimson lake liveries.

Another 2P of 1928 No. 40569 and a BR Standard Class 5 head a north-bound train shortly after leaving Winsor Hill Tunnel.

DEFEATED BY THE DRAINS

Stephen Spark

That unfinished business, the Chessington branch, has been admirably covered in *Southern Way* nos 26 and 27, but there is more to tell.

Jeremy Clarke (*SW* 26) pointed to the stimulus the Kingston Bypass provided for house-building, but 13 months before the road opened the London Passenger Transport Board began running trains on the Northern Line's southern extension. Morden was designed as a through station and it was envisaged that the Northern would continue towards North Cheam and Sutton, but it could equally have headed south-west to Leatherhead. The station forecourt soon became a hub for feeder bus services that started cutting into the Southern's commuter traffic. As the population grew, the local authorities pressed LPTB to build a duplicate tube line between Kennington and Morden, which could be extended out to Epsom. The Southern was under attack, and the Chessington branch was quite possibly the last railway to have been built as a 'blocking' line to prevent further Tube encroachments into its territory.

Both LPTB and the SR kept quiet about their expansion plans, but by 1929 Surbiton Council realised something was afoot and asked the Southern if there was truth in the "persistent rumours" that a station was to be built at Tolworth. The SR denied any such plan and suggested the rumours related to an Underground extension from Morden. In May, F A Pinfold, assistant to the General Manager, mentioned "the proposed new line from Motspur Park to Leatherhead" in a memo, but the council only learned the truth in October. The town clerk protested to SR General Manager Sir Herbert Walker that the council had not been given the chance to comment on the plans and "keenly resent the way they have been treated by the Railway Company". Walker harrumphed: "I… strongly resent the tone [of the letter] and the imputations contained therein" and demanded the clerk withdraw his letter before he would give an explanation. However, the clerk bested him by copying the correspondence to the Ministry of Transport, so Walker was forced to excuse himself by saying there had been too little time to consult with "the various town planning authorities involved". In fact, only two councils were affected and, as we have seen, the SR had had five months to discuss the proposals with them. The SR was clearly playing its cards very close to its chest, possibly for fear of a counter-attack by the LPTB and speculation by property developers. However, Walker's personality probably played a part, too. According to Charles Klapper, "He had an instinctive fear of disclosing plans prematurely [1]."

The next major development in the area proved to be a welcome one for the SR: the purchase of an old mansion, Burnt Stub, by millionaire animal collector Reginald Goddard. In July 1931 he opened the grounds to the public as the Surrey Zoological Gardens, and the zoo proved to be a lucrative source of traffic for many years.

As usual, the Southern planned its new line as economically as possible. One of the rotary converters for Chessington South rectifier sub-station was a 1924 unit recovered from Leatherhead RSS, and cabling from the Leatherhead-Effingham Junction line was reused along the new branch. However, the line's construction prompted major expenditure on resignalling of the main line between Hampton Court Junction and Waterloo and construction of the Wimbledon flyover.

In 1934 it was estimated that five eight-coach trains would be needed for the new services to Chessington South, comprising ten three-car motor sets and five two-car trailer sets. If the line were to be extended to Leatherhead, a further pair of eight-coach trains would be required. The total cost of 12 complete trains would be £168,980, but this could be reduced by £26,660 if the three-coach units were converted from steam-hauled stock.

The local clay was useful raw material for the brickyards at Tolworth, Malden Rushett and Woodbridge (Leatherhead), but, as mentioned by Mike King in *SW* 27, it proved troublesome for civil engineers. The presence of corrosive sulphates and the intractable physical properties of the clay rendered excavated material all but useless for creating embankments elsewhere on the line, so Benjamin Cloke was contracted to remove McAlpine's spoil to a tip in an old gravel pit at Teddington. Cloke was also responsible for bringing in the new fill material, which came from slum clearance in north and east London and carted via the Blackwall Tunnel to a specially constructed loading dock at Bricklayers Arms.

Several changes were made to the station layouts as construction progressed. In anticipation of heavy traffic, it was decided to build side platforms rather than Wimbledon-Sutton-style islands. A proposed goods shed at Tolworth was cancelled, with smalls traffic being handled by Surbiton and carted from there. A suggestion to run the words "Southern Railway" vertically down the lift shafts – which if spelled out in Odeon-style neon would have looked rather striking – was not carried out, and the planned footbridge at Chessington South was indefinitely postponed, although one can still see the blocked aperture for it in the platform wall of the station building. Rather surprisingly, the 'ghost' platform canopy on the up line at South is still cleaned and painted every so often.

With the exception of Tolworth, the stations proved difficult to name to everyone's satisfaction. Maldon Manor was originally proposed as Old Malden. Chessington

North started out as Hook (a far more accurate name and less likely to cause confusion), although both Moor Lane and Chessington Grange were in vogue for a while. Chessington South was to have been plain Chessington or Church Lane (the road itself was renamed Garrison Lane before the line's opening). If Goddard had prevailed, the terminus would have been called Chessington Zoo. Eustace Missenden, traffic manager, protested: "I do not think that such a name as 'Chessington Zoo' would be regarded with favour by the present inhabitants of the neighbourhood or the prospective residents." Goddard continued to complain, politely, about the proposed names of Chessington Court and Chessington Grange – the one did not exist, he pointed out, while the other was "a house which could not have cost more than £1,000" and would be demolished as soon as the railway arrived. Missenden eventually came round to Goddard's view that Court and Grange would not do, and in January 1939 the railway, council and zoo all agreed that they could live with North and South instead.

The two stations planned for the Leatherhead extension were referred to as Rushet Lane (at Malden Rushett) and Leatherhead Gap or Leatherhead North, at the southern extremity of Ashtead Common and just north of the present M25 interchange.

Colonel A C Trench, in his inspection report of 25 May 1939, was impressed with the two Chessington stations: "The passenger arrangements appear to be well designed and convenient and the buildings are attractive in appearance… The platform roofs are of the same patent half arch type as those of the other two stations on the line but with the ribs outside instead of inside." Trench noted that there was one footpath crossing, which would shortly be removed, fencing was of the new Peerless chain link type and ARP (air raid precautions) shelters were provided in the subway at North and at platform level at South.

The concrete canopies at the stations were indeed revolutionary. Chisarc was a trade name used by T A Chisholm, who traded as Architectural Services Ltd and was UK licensee of the reinforced concrete shell system patented in 1920 by Carl Zeiss (better known for high-quality camera lenses) and Dyckerhoff & Widmann (D&W), hence it was known as the Zeiss Dywidag system. The first concrete shell roof in Britain was erected in 1936 at Doncaster Municipal Airport[2], so it was rather courageous of SR chief engineer George Ellson to adopt the system just a few months later for the new stations. Chisholm said the canopies could be erected in three months, which Ellson told the board had "definite advantages over any [offer] we should receive from steelwork contractors". D&W diplomatically tried to dissuade Ellson from insisting on platform valances – one has a mental image of a German designer spluttering with indignation that the tea-drinking Anglo-Philistines were going to spoil the Bauhaus purity of his canopy with frilly fretwork! Although Malden Manor and Tolworth do have plain valances, the Chessington canopies are unvalanced.

The lack of supports certainly de-cluttered the platform in an elegant way, but unfortunately Ellson was unduly optimistic when he asserted that the canopies had "the advantage of avoiding periodical expensive repainting". In pristine condition Malden Manor and Tolworth looked striking, but quickly became dismal when neglected. This may explain why Ellson decided that the second pair of stations should be finished with facing bricks rather than Brizolite rendering. Like Chisarc, Brizolite was of German origin and was introduced to the UK by the celebrated founder of the Bauhaus movement, Professor Walter Gropius[3]. The Southern's engineers seem to have been reading all the trendy architectural magazines! Sir Herbert Walker was disappointed with the shift to brick, telling Ellson, "The appearance of the stations which have been finished is quite agreeable." The CE merely replied: "It will be more satisfactory to use a facing brick at the two stations."

In May 1938, Walker's successor as GM, Gilbert Szlumper, congratulated Chisholm, saying, "I like the Chessington line stations and look on them as an auspicious start" – which rather suggests that more examples might have been built had the war and nationalisation not intervened.

The fluorescent tubes in the canopies were originally pink/amber and blue/white, which combined to give an approximation of daylight[4], showing the attention to detail expended on the Chessington branch stations. This was, after all, at a time when gas lighting was still common, and a few miles away at Cook's Crossing on the New Line, electrified since 1925, the signal box continued to be gaslit until the 1970s. The fluorescent lighting had a higher first cost but was expected to consume less power – an early example of energy-saving lighting.

The desire to reduce ongoing maintenance costs was apparent in that decision to encase steel plate girder bridges in concrete, but in this case the logic is harder to follow. The Southern, as we know, was an enthusiastic adopter of concrete; indeed, it was probably the UK's first major mass-producer of large precast reinforced concrete (RC) structures, and its concrete footbridges were really the precursors of 'system building'. Given this heritage, it is surprising that Ellson did not opt for all-concrete bridges on the line. By this time, reinforced concrete was being widely used for highway overbridges – including several on the Kingston Bypass.

The most southerly of those bridges was the part-completed structure over Chalky Lane beyond Chessington South, which seems never to have received its concrete overcoat (illustrated in *SW* 26). It was still in place when an aerial photograph was taken of the area in 1948[5].

The Leatherhead extension is a fascinating 'might have been'. It was envisaged from the start, but it was to be built on what *The Railway Gazette* called "the telescopic principle", in which railway construction would progress stage by stage, keeping pace with housing development.

That development never happened. But why not, and why did the line never get beyond the headshunt of Charrington's coal yard? The conventional answers are (i) the outbreak of war and (ii) the imposition of Green Belt planning restrictions. Both are true, up to a point, but do not tell the whole story. In fact the line was sunk by sewerage.

With the exception of the gaudy delights of Chessington World of Adventures, a clutch of houses and some low-key light industry at Malden Rushett, the area between Chalky Lane and the M25 interchange north of Leatherhead remains almost entirely undeveloped. This is not for want of trying on successive developers' part. Taking the Malden Rushett crossroads as the centre point, peaceful fields surround Park Farm to the north-east; Rushett Farm to the south-east is frequented by skylark, lapwing and yellowhammer, beyond which lie Epsom and Ashtead Commons; the Crown Estate own Byhurst Farm to the south-west, with Prince's Coverts and Stoke Wood extending westwards almost to the Guildford New Line; and more fields and woods surround World of Adventures in the north-west quadrant. Yet had the developers been able to realise their schemes, Malden Rushett crossroads would today look like Tolworth – which is not a recommendation.

As early as 1895, the owners of Byhurst Farm were planning to sell the land for housing development, but public transport links were poor. Residents of Chessington and Hook petitioned the LSWR in 1906 to run a motor bus service from Surbiton and received the usual laconic "to be declined[6]". Seven years later, there was an unsuccessful proposal to extend Kingston's electric tramways down to Leatherhead.

The trams never arrived, but aircraft did. During the First World War, a Royal Flying Corps landing ground was established just west of the present site of Chessington South station. The land was later occupied by a Second World War barrage balloon station and government offices, and it is now a housing estate. That was not the end of flying, however, because William Chapman set up Leatherhead Air Services at Byhurst Farm to offer people pleasure flights around the Surrey countryside in a DH 6 and three Avro 504Ks. After several crashes, the business folded in 1922[7], but some years later an airfield was established next to the Kingston Bypass at Hook[8].

By now, the local councils had caught the flying bug and wanted some aviation action for themselves. In March 1935, Sir Herbert Walker learned to his horror that Kingston and Surbiton councils planned to establish a fully fledged aerodrome at Byhurst Farm – right in the centre of the catchment area for the proposed Malden Rushett station. Walker wrote to the Kingston town clerk: "The company view with very much concern the proposal to establish the Aerodrome in this position, particularly for the reason that they have been encouraged to promote and construct the railway on assurance that the districts through which it would pass, and Chessington in particular, would be planned and developed mainly for housing purposes."

You might imagine the SR would have been delighted at the prospect of an airport, and all the traffic it would bring, right next to its new line. After all, in that same year the company had opened stations at Shoreham Airport and Tinsley Green (for Gatwick Airport). However, Walker sternly reminded the clerk, "The existence of an Aerodrome has an extremely detrimental effect upon the amenities of the surrounding property and most seriously affects the development of the neighbourhood which becomes practically sterilized, so far as housing development is concerned, for an area of some two miles round the Aerodrome." The SR might have to cancel construction of the line, he warned. Even the prescient Walker could hardly have foreseen the effect that cheap foreign holidays were going to have on numbers of passengers using London's airports three decades later.

The proposal was, in any event, a curious one, because a covenant of the previous year had expressly forbidden the development of the Byhurst land as an aerodrome. Nevertheless, to test its practicability, or perhaps just for fun, B H Turner in September 1934 attempted a parachute descent on to the proposed Kingston and Surbiton Aerodrome. Unfortunately, he drifted off course and landed on top of the lion cage at Chessington Zoo! Somehow he evaded the lions' attempts to grab his legs and was pulled to safety by the keeper[9].

The excitement subsided and Chessington did not, after all, become London's second airport, although thrill-seekers can still take helicopter rides from a small airstrip on the other side of Leatherhead Road at Rushett Farm. Six flying days a year are hardly enough to justify a 'Chessington Express' airport service, though!

Prospective housebuilders quickly moved in and submitted their plans for Byhurst Farm. At the north end of the extension route the council went into partnership with builders to develop the Chessington Hall estate, while to the south-west the Crown Estate, in its leisurely way, formulated plans to develop its vast holdings between the Guildford New Line and the southern limb of the Chessington branch. Another developer offered the SR a £1,000 sweetener if it would push on quickly down to Malden Rushett.

It was all going swimmingly… until Surbiton Council started asking for contributions for improving the area's sewerage system and pumping station. Drains and water supply in this largely undeveloped area would be unable to cope with a massive increase in population. The get-rich-quick developers had not factored infrastructure costs in to their calculations. As the delays grew and the correspondence files thickened, the speculators lost interest. And then war was declared.

Work continued for a while, nonetheless, so in 1941 chalk removed from Basingtoke for new sidings at Up West Yard was taken down to (appropriately enough) Chalky Lane[10]. Alan Jackson states that the embankment was extended southwards by the Royal Engineers as a training exercise[11], which is plausible, but I have been unable to confirm this. Local residents suggested that some work may also have been carried out by Italian prisoners of war who were billeted in the area.

The struggle to secure the route from rapacious speculators had forced the Southern into more expense than it had bargained for, so it was understandable that it was reluctant to surrender this hard-won territory. Doubtless

Gilbert Szlumper and Eustace Missenden hoped that conditions would return to normal after the conflict. However, the Abercrombie Report, which proposed the Green Belt, and the Town & Country Planning Act of 1943 that enshrined those protections in law, put paid to that idea. It was not for want of trying on the part of the London County Council, which in November 1945 proposed what Surbiton Borough Council called a "misconceived" proposal to build a 670-acre "satellite town" centred on Malden Rushett, rehousing bombed-out Londoners from the East End. The council and the local MP lobbied successfully for the plan to be thrown out – not least on the grounds that the sewers would never cope!

By January 1946, the estimated cost of completion to Leatherhead had risen by 75% to £660,000 and the board decided: "At the present time there was no justification for proceeding with the extension and the future prospects of development were uncertain."

Before the war Goddard had discussed with the SR the possibility of running a light railway from Chessington South (perhaps the unused up platform) along the embankment to a new halt at Chalky Lane. Southern Region PR officer Cuthbert Grasemann was enthusiastic when the zoo dusted off the proposal in 1949. This was presumably so the zoo could convey more passengers than were able to squeeze into the antique horse-drawn knifeboard bus it had operated since 1947. The zoo was to provide the light railway and its equipment, and British Railways would offer through ticketing. Grasemann wrote in a memo to the chief regional officer, "It is a weary trail for mothers and children after a long day at the zoo… to have to trudge along the road for over half a mile to the station." Having done just that on more than one occasion, the author can only agree wholeheartedly! The chief engineer estimated the cost of the new line and the halt, exclusive of signalling, at £6,000, and the light railway was expected to contribute an additional £1,000 in revenue annually. Sadly, the line never materialised.

Nevertheless, the zoo was rail-served in its own, rather idiosyncratic, way. Goddard had started out with a 2ft gauge Bagnall 0-4-0ST that operated on a 100-yard length of track, but the engine proved rather a liability and was swiftly replaced by a bizarre scratchbuilt 12in gauge petrol tractor cobbled together from parts of a Vimy bomber and powered by a Triumph motorcycle engine. For the 1932 season, a second loco was assembled from bits of another Vimy and the engine and gearbox from a Citroën car. More incarnations appeared using Vimy and Citroën components, but in 1937 Norwich-based engineering firm Barnards created two fine 12in-gauge GWR Dukedogs powered by Austin 10 car engines, which hauled many thousands of children around the zoo until the railway's closure in 1984 [12]. Today there is no railway and very few visitors to the World of Adventures arrive by train.

Beyond its gates a line of trees marks the course of the ill-fated Leatherhead extension. It would be interesting to know who owns the land, which is virtually untouched. Exmouth Junction concrete posts and remnants of wire can

still be found along this linear woodland. The embankment was continued well beyond Chalky Lane and rudimentary earthworks can be found in Chessington Wood, just north of Rushett Lane, which the line would have crossed on a bridge, not on the level. Through Ashtead Common, the line would have been in a cutting (more spoil to remove!), descending for almost a mile at 1 in 90 to Leatherhead North station. After crossing the small River Rye, the line, which up to this point was to have followed a consistent south-westerly course, swung first to the south and then to the west on 2 furlong-radius curves. It would have joined the Epsom line just under the public footbridge leading to the Kingston Road recreation ground.

Quite how three extra trains each way per hour off the Chessington branch were to be accommodated at Leatherhead is a puzzle that the surviving records do not seem to address. Two options suggest themselves: the service might have been carried on to Effingham Junction, where there were turnround facilities and a seven-road carriage shed; or Leatherhead's old LSWR station might have been spruced up and pressed into service once again. The latter had been closed only in 1927, when all services were concentrated on the LBSC station, and the tracks and platforms remained in use for berthing and cleaning stock until the 1970s. The third option, creating a bay at the London end of the LBSC station, would have necessitated major reorganisation of the goods yard.

The unused embankment in the woods continues to excite the imaginations of transport planners. Although powers to build the railway lapsed in 1961, the land remained zoned for transport use in the Surrey Development Plan for many decades. In 1995 Surrey County Council suggested the alignment could be used for an extension to Horton, which lies to the south-east of Chessington South. From 1905 to 1950 this vast London County Council hospital complex was served by the Horton Estate Light Railway, which ran off a siding on the up side of the Epsom to Raynes Park line just south of Ewell West station [13]. Much of the site has been redeveloped for housing. Ten years later, the Green Party recommended extending from the present terminus to a station opposite Chessington World of Adventures and then veering off south-eastwards to Epsom via the hospitals site. The proposal was supported in principle by the Royal Borough of Kingston-upon-Thames. At about the same time, South London Trams suggested a tramway from Kingston through Tolworth, Chessington and Malden Rushett to the M25 Leatherhead interchange – essentially a re-run of the 1913 proposal. A subsequent report by Halcrow recommended against it.

In 1952 an electric tram did reach Chessington. Privately preserved London Transport tram no 1858 sat in a field at the zoo until 1968, when it was moved to the East Anglia Transport Museum at Carlton Colville, where it can be seen today.

It is just conceivable that trams may one day run south of Chessington, but it seems very unlikely that we will see class 455s or their successors running along that embankment and descending through the wooded cuttings of Ashtead Common into Leatherhead. But birdwatchers do have the consolation of knowing that they may hear a nightingale in the fields behind Malden Rushett…

Notes and references

The greater part of the information for this article has been taken from National Archives series RAIL 1188/112, 115, 116 and 117 on the Chessington branch; RAIL 645/106 Inspections of new works; AN 157/88 Proposed extension to Chalky Lane for zoo; CRES 38/2024 Byhurst Farm. Material consulted at Kingston Archives included KT 82/10/7 newspaper cuttings; KT 107/S43/1 and S44/1 on the railway and its bridges. At the Surrey History Centre can be found the deposited plans and books of reference QS6/8/1720 and 1722; CC 124/11 Satellite town at Chessington; J00081 00067 *LDLHS Newsletter* Mar 2001 'The railway that never arrived'; *SIHG Newsletter* nos 161 (1/2008) and 162 (3/2008) 'Leatherhead Aviation Services'. My thanks go to staff at TNA, SHC and Kingston Archives, local residents' associations in Chessington and Leatherhead and also the Leatherhead & District Local History Society.

Specific references (1-13) are listed below.

Klapper, C F: *Sir Herbert Walker's Southern Railway* (1973), p 13

Cement & Concrete Association (1950). *Concrete shell and barrel roofs*. London: Cement & Concrete Association
Country Life, 23 Oct 2009 (www.countrylife.co.uk/news/property-news/flat-by-the-founder-of-the-bauhaus)
'New Southern Railway suburban line', *The Railway Gazette*, 27 May 1938
Surrey History Centre, CC 1103/3/1/58
Traffic Committee minute no 153 of 16 May 1906, National Archives RAIL 411/267
Peter Tarplee: 'Leatherhead Aviation Services', *Proc Leatherhead & District Local History Society*, vol 7, no 1, 2007
Kingston Archives, Aviation file D2/26
'A parachute thrill', *Flight*, 20 Sep 1934
National Archives RAIL 1188/230
Alan Jackson: 'Chessington – Southern suburban swansong', *The Railway Magazine*, Jan 1974
Ken Bean: 'The Bower Brothers build a railway', *The Heywood Society Journal*, no 52, Spring 2003
C G Down: 'Horton Estate Light Railway', *The Industrial Railway Record*, no 13, Mar 1967

Note: On page 101 of SW29 the last few words of text were unfortunately omitted. The end of the sentence should read, "...to where the underframes were built."

Book Review

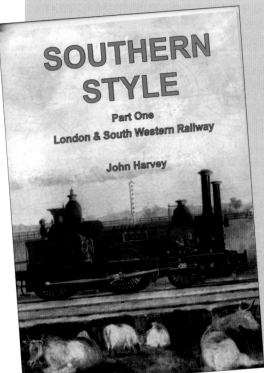

A copy of 'Southern Style, Part One, London & South Western Railway' by John Harvey, published by the Historical Model Railway Society, arrived on the doorstep in late January. Up to now I think the number of book reviews that have appeared in 'SW' can probably be counted on the fingers of one hand – with some to spare as well – but this had to be an exception to the rule.

I had heard rumours that the original LSWR/Southern Livery Register was to be undated and looked forward very much to the result.

For those not aware, the first book was compiled by Len Tavender in 1970 and afforded a most useful guide to painting and colour schemes as well as headcodes at various periods as well as a colour chart. If it suffered from anything it was the constraints of the time - although I still have a well-thumbed copy on the shelf.

This new book is an A4 paperback of 124 sides, mainly b/w with a few colour inclusions mainly at the start and end of the book. It incorporates a stiff colour fold-out, 'Specimen Colour Samples', as a separate inclusion.

The book is arranged is an easy to follow style with, after a general introduction, sections and sub-sections on 'The Application of the Livery', and also actual 'Colours'. A section on references and an index are also included.

This is a revision that has been needed for some time. Whilst there may be some who will immediately read it from cover to cover, I personally tend to dip in to various sections which of course then tend to lead to another, and another.....a wonderful way to spend (my wife would say waste) an evening, but then she indulges in her own interests. I should add almost the only omission from the original is the aforementioned head-codes, but then this new book does not profess to be an 'operating' guide so it should not be criticised.

The final pages refer to a second volume by Peter Wisdon to come in Summer 2015. This will be on the 'London, Brighton & South Coast Railway.'

I can do no more than highly recommend what is an excellent publication.

£27.50 ISBN 978-0-902835-31-3

(NB – Speaking to Mike King, he advises me work is progressing on a separate 'Southern Railway' volume. I would personally hope the SECR will also be covered in the future.)

SOUTHERN RAILWAY
TRAFFIC OFFICERS CONFERENCE:

Minutes of a meeting held at Waterloo Station on Monday 28 March 1938 chaired by Gilbert Szlumper CBE General Manager

(Notes compiled by David Monk-Steel)

- continued from Issue No 28

10352   Working of Freight Trains. For the month of February –
DEPARTURES

DIVISION	Total Number of trains run , (including Specials)	Average minutes late departure	Average number of wagons per train
London East	4194	1.2	28.8
London Central	3938	1.3	27.9
London West	4444	1.6	38.2
Southern	1292	0.9	24.4
Western	1247	1.5	20.5
TOTAL	15115	1.4	30.3

ARRIVALS

DIVISION	Total Number of trains run , (including Specials)	Average minutes late departure	Average number of wagons per train
London East	4118	5.9	27.7
London Central	3837	5.8	28.1
London West	4478	9.7	36.1
Southern	1248	2.2	24.0
Western	1208	3.1	20.4
TOTAL	14889	6.5	29.7

Fog on 24th & 25th February, Snow on 15th & 16th February
10353 **Trains failing to call at Stations** February 1938: Steam - 4, Electric – 8

10354   Points, Signal and Track Circuit Failures

Division	No. of Failures	Minutes Delay
London (East)	156	627½
London (Central)	229	1304
London (West)	149	483½
Southern	22	71
Western	12	99
TOTAL for February	568	2585

111

10355   Continental Traffic

Southern Railway Co Steamers

PORT	No of passengers	Tons of Cargo	Motor Cars
Southampton	4422	3300	85
Dover & Folkestone	51573	7065	812
Newhaven	8176	1921	242

Other Company's Steamers

PORT	No of passengers	Tons of Cargo	Motor Cars
Dover (Belgian Marine)	13665	428	125
Gravesend (Batavia)	576	-	-

Dover to Dunkerque Ferry

February 1938

Passengers Sleeping Car 1st	Passengers Sleeping Car 2nd	Passengers Ordinary 1st	Passengers Ordinary 2nd	Tons of Cargo	Wagons loaded	Wagons empty
1312	1117	305	685	5285	1469	945

Principal goods carried February 1938
Dover to Dunkerque -   1466 tons of Wool,
Dunkerque to Dover -   1376 tons of fruit and vegetables
                                            506 tons poultry
                                            226 tons of machinery
                                            170 tons of Woollens & Cottons
                                            161 tons of flowers
All other commodities in loads less than 100 tons in total for the month.
Sailings cancelled 8th February due to fog (2), 13th and 15th February due to gales (5).

10357   Isle of Wight Passenger and Motor Car Traffic

	Passengers	Motor Cars
Portsmouth	58597	475
Lymington	2905	32

Members of the Institute of Locomotive Engineers at Chart Leacon being shown the de-icing arrangements on a former SUB unit. Mr S B Warder, then president of the ILE is pointing to the delivery pipe.

10358   **Comparative Return of railway traffic receipts for the four companies**
11 weeks ended the 20th March 1938

	SOUTHERN	GW	LM&S	L&NE
Passenger	**£2,395,300**	£1,204,000	£2,996,100	£1,966,900
Parcels etc.	**£446,700**	£595,000	£1,295,900	£885,100
Merchandise	**£650,500**	£2,189,000	£5,363,000	£3,753,000
Coal & Coke	**£413,500**	£1,386,000	£3,369,000	£3,086,000

10360   Ramblers Excursions

In 1937 55 excursions requiring 73 trains were run for Ramblers. 28,916 ramblers were carried and the average number of passengers per train was 396. This traffic earned £5,569 in receipts.

10361   Circular Tours

Receipts for Circular Tours in 1937 was £22769 / 16s / 9d .

10362   Holiday Camping Coaches

CREDITS					DEBITS				
	1935 £	1936 £	1937 £	TOTAL £		1935 £	1936 £	1937 £	TOTAL £
RENTALS	673	763	871	2307					
Rail Tickets receipts from rom Tenants of camping coaches	1074	1117	1287	3478	Residual value of 12 no. Type 'B' Coaches (£264) on basis of 10 year life	26	26	26	78
					Residual value of 6 type 'A' coaches (£226) on basis of 10 years life	-	23	23	46
					Conversion and equipment of 12 type 'B' coaches (£1862) on the basis of 10 years life	186	186	186	558
					Interest on Capital	93	93	93	279
					Conversion and equipment of 6 type 'A' coaches (£1316) on the basis of 10 years life		132	132	264
					Interest on Capital		66	66	66
					Repairs	14	123	136	273
					Laundry	48	53	57	158
					Printing and Advertising	136	123	65	324
					Hire of Crockery	4	8	8	20
					Miscellaneous	25	6	10	41
TOTAL	1747	1880	2158	5785	TOTAL	532	839	802	2173

10363   Football traffic at Twickenham

England v Scotland 19th March 1938.
Bookings from Waterloo   17,066
No. of tickets collected at Waterloo and Twickenham 28,533
Approximate number of return passengers   32,660
50 trains run (ordinary and special) between 11:45am and 2:30 pm from Waterloo to Twickenham,
35 trains run (ordinary and special) between 4:30pm and 6:30 pm from Twickenham to Waterloo.

10364 Development committee

The following matters were dealt with at the meeting on 15th March 1938.

General Motors Ltd. Southampton

In the face of low "drive away" charges, competitive rates are being quoted to various destinations to increase rail carryings of Opel cars now being imported via Southampton on account of this firm.

Industrial Estate at Ford Junction

Reported that about 300 acres of land adjacent to Ford station are to be laid out for industrial development, the proposal being to erect factories for light industry and small houses on 'Garden City' lines. The traffic Manager is in touch with the promoter.

Express Dairy Co. Ltd

This firm has decided to rent a site at New Cross Gate for the erection of a milk depot to serve south east London. A rental of £200 per annum has been agreed and the dairy company is preparing plans. This should lead to a considerable increase in milk traffic.

Seager and Evans & Co. Ltd. Distillers

This firm has rented about one acre of land at Blackheath Hill station, on which they propose to erect a store. The rental is £150 per annum.

10365 Salaries and Wages Expenditure

Monthly Paid Salaries	£ 12,320
Weekly Paid Salaries and Wages	
Locomotive Running	£142,808
Electric Running	£ 21,868
Traffic	£324,531
Police	£ 6,168
Horse	£ 1,830

SOUTHERN RAILWAY TRAFFIC OFFICERS CONFERENCE: 28 March 1938

10366   Staff Changes
10367   Hours of Duty of certain grades of staff in the Traffic, Locomotive and Electrical departments
10368   Detection by staff of Irregular Travelling

10369   Staff Punishments
Statements were presented to the Committee and the four topics above were discussed but fully detailed minutes were not published.

10370 Staff 60 years of age and over
25 salaried staff were listed as attaining 60 years before the end of May 1938, 8 were to be superannuated, and the rest retained for the present.

10371   Combined Rail and Road Bookings etc. Associated Road Companies
Additional facilities have been introduced –
Maidstone and District Motor Services - a joint monthly season ticket from Bearstead to Charing and then by road from Charing (Post Office) to Lord Romney's Hill
Southdown Motor Services – a joint Quarterly combined season ticket rate available from London and Rottingdean (Chailey Avenue) via Brighton.

10372   Post Office Telephone Facilities
Additional telephone facilities authorised for –
Barming station, Malden Manor and Tolworth (new stations), Portsmouth Arms (loud sounding bell to enable the signalman to hear the bell), Victoria Continental Enquiry Office, extra line for Tourist Agents.

10373   Conveyance of Milk in Tank wagons for the Express Dairy Company
The Traffic Manager has received an application from the Express Dairy Company for the provision of a 6,000 gallon capacity tank wagon consisting of two 3,000 gallon tanks mounted upon a bogie underframe, the whole being covered by an 'all over streamlined ' design. The tanks and canopy will be provided by the Dairy Company. The cost of the wagon is estimated as £550, which will be charged to the Carriage Renewal reserve. The application is recommended for approval.

10374   Barnstaple Junction – Saw Milling and General Supplies Co Siding
The terms of the agreement with the firm in respect of this siding have been under re-negotiation, terms for maintaining the siding are now finalised.

10375   Guildford – Proposed siding to serve the Guildford Pure Ice Company's siding.
Further to Minute 9756 of 16th November 1936 the firm have decided not to go ahead with this proposal.

10376   Merton Abbey, Proposed access between the goods yard and factory of Messrs A. & A.J. Law Ltd.
The firm are requesting direct road access from their proposed factory premises in Littlers Close to the Goods Yard. An initial payment of £25 for the Company to make the access, and an agreement to then pay over the next ten years £2 / 10s / 0d per annum if the total tonnage of goods to the railway falls below 400 tons. The agreement is recommended.

10377 Charge for Workmen's compensation included in accounts for work done for outside parties by the Engineer's department
The charges for "Labour" shall in future be amended to read – "Actual cost, plus 20% to cover the various on-costs including Workmen's compensation". This is in accordance with a standard agreement for bridges recommended by the Ministry of Transport.

10378   New Works
The following New Works are recommended -

Station etc.	Nature of Work	Estimated cost
Balcombe	Proposed new booking office at road level	£314
Bexleyheath	Proposed new goods office	£342
Bournemouth Central Goods	Temporary dock for Royal County Show traffic	£327
Nine Elms	Alterations to roadway in Brooklands Yard	£350
Pevensey Bay Halt	Provision of wheel for automatic closing of level crossing gates	£850
Southampton Central	Improved accommodation for station staff	£284
Strawberry Hill	Accommodation for guards and motormen at the station	£480
Victoria (Continental Enquiry Office)	Improvements to counter space, new cupboards, and small automatic telephone circuit.	£400
Waterloo	Extension of telephone switchboard to accommodate 50 additional lines	£720

Terry Cole's Rolling Stock File No. 30
Isle of Wight Goods Stock (1)

The Isle of Wight system maintained its 'period charm' right to the end of steam operation. So far as its goods vehicles were concerned, none of the BR standard designs reached the Island, the most modern being of Southern Railway origin with most being considerably older. There was in fact minimal goods traffic apart from coal from Medina Wharf and Engineers' Trains. Vehicles often saw little use and were well maintained so there was no need to replace them.

Above - This lovely train of wagons is being shunted at Medina Wharf by an immaculate No. W31 'Chale'. The ex LSWR Diagram 1541 brake van No. S56057 is in unfitted BR grey livery as are two of the 5 plank wagons. The SR 8-plank wagon nearest the camera appears to be in faded SR brown.

Opposite top - No. S56046, a double ended ex LSWR Diagram 1542 brake van with side ducket, is seen at Ryde St Johns Road. A relatively recent arrival, it was not shipped over to the Island until 1948. It was however built back in 1906 as a six wheeler. Next to it is ex LBSCR 12ft.Single Bolster wagon No. DS 59045 of diagram 1616. None of these brake vans appears to have a stove. The journeys were probably too short to bother.

Opposite bottom - A similar brake van, No. S56046 is seen here in the coal siding at Cowes, this time still carrying its SR brown paintwork. A Bedford 'TK', the typical coal merchants and modern general haulage road lorry of the time reposes behind.

Images Terry Cole collection (above and opposite top), and Terry Cole.).

The Funeral Train of Sir Winston Churchill

Probably like many readers of 'SW', I recall watching the funeral of Sir Winston Churchill on television in January 1965. Calculating the years back I recall watching it avidly (on a 17-inch 'Echo' 405 line TV). The day was a Saturday. It would leave a lasting impression, a memory rekindled more recently with various programmes to commemorate 50 years on that were broadcast in January.

As a publisher I have also had the privilege of meeting Jim Lester, fireman on the actual train as well publishing his memories (covering his whole railway life) a few years ago under the title, 'Southern Engineman'*.

In January 2015 I received a note from Michael Roach, "I sent these two pictures to a friend recently. He takes *The Southern Way* and recommended that I ought to send them to you in case you do an article on the subject of Sir Winston Churchill's Funeral train. They are not brilliant, but it was quite a dull bleak day where I was when the train passed. They were taken about a mile north of Culham Station and just before the train passed over the River Thames at Nuneham Bridge. I had travelled from my home in Plymouth to be there for these two photographs." (All I can say is 'thank you', it is a pleasure to include them - Ed.)

A few days later I also received one of Terry Bye's regular 'Pullman' e-newsletters (well worth subscribing to as well). This included a feature on how the PMV used in the train as the actual funeral van was selected, one might almost say plucked from obscurity. Again with thanks to Terry, Glen Woods and others mentioned, an extract is now reproduced. Readers will be aware the van itself and the cosmetically restored No 34051 are at the time of writing on

display at the National Railway Museum.

"This report comes from the "carbon copy" of the Rolling Stock Inspector's report contained in a book (BR 206/3 I believe). This and other material was in the Frank Davis collection purchased by the Bluebell Railway Museum Archive.

Frank was well known in BR circles and scrounged anything he could (including from me!) and thanks be that he did. I have this (and other items from the Frank Davis collection) on loan in my position as an Assistant Archivist. I shall check the original to see if the name of the RSI is given at the end of the report. Sgnd.: Glen Woods.

Rolling Stock Inspector's Report: Bogie Luggage Vans Worthy Down 3rd July 1962.

Van No. 2464 - 16 Tons, Rest "0", 53' body.

(Worthy Down was on the erstwhile Didcot, Newbury & Southampton line, but the carriage storage that took place there was not at the station. This was on the former WW2 spur that had once linked the SR and GWR between Winchester Junction and Worthy Down. One end of this (the SR end) was severed in 1950 leaving a long siding - 1 mile or so long - trailing back from Worthy Down. Vehicles were stored here pending works visit or scrapping).

Of the 24 Vans berthed on the single line at Worthy Down I have selected Van No. 2464 as the best of a poor lot, requiring the least amount of repair to make it presentable, the canvas covered roof is in a reasonably good condition, the body panels are reasonably good and the decalite

THE FUNERAL TRAIN OF SIR WINSTON CHURCHILL

floor in good order. The underframe headstocks are thin and bent behind the buffers but the bogies are fairly good. It will, of course, require lifting and painting inside and out. The gangway diaphragms are perished but the frames and scissors are fairly sound. All the cells and dynamo are intact and appear in good condition. The main steam and vacuum pipes require testing, the lagging from the former is adrift in places. Berthing position at Worthy Down: Winchester Junction end, line broken No Entry or Exit." (Further discussion on the van selected appears in the 'Editorial' on p5.)

Last Paint date: 9/56, Crimson Lake Livery	
Body -	Panels reasonably sound. Exterior paint bad – peeling off. Interior paint bad – peeling off
Floor -	Decalite good condition
Gangways -	BS(A) – diaphragms perished. Scissors, face plates sound metal extension frame – slight buckle at bottom corners
Underframes -	Steel Headstocks bent behind the four side buffers. Solebar flanges are thin Wood main members, sound and dry
Bogies -	Press Steel – reasonably good. Wheels 9" X 4" Steel Disc, Tyres 2¾" profile good
Mountings -	Either side screw brake operative. 2 vacuum cylinders, main pipe and steam pipes require testing. 22" oval face buffers, gedge draw gear
Since berthing 11 of the 16 door and fixed lights have been broken and wiring exposed	

6586 BCK Set 26	5646 CK Set 270	2354 Cor-PMV	2487 Cor-PMV	1248 SK Set 269
1254 SK Loose	1226 SK Set 270	2282 Cor-PMV	2333 Cor-PMV	5691 CK Set 269
1204 SK Loose	830 SK Set 205	2482 Cor-PMV	2476 Cor-PMV	1806 SK Set269
1921 SK Loose	1123 SK Set 205	2308 Cor-PMV	2488 Cor-PMV n	1228 SK Loose
1247 SK Set 432	3230 BSK) Set 398	2465 Cor-PMV	2331 Cor-PMV	1269 SK Loose
1840 SK Loose	5144 CK) No Inter	2305 Cor-PMV	2344 Cor-PMV	7231 First Set 442
1250 SK Set 201	3227 BSK) Buffers	2337 Cor-PMV	2290 Cor-PMV	1399 SO Set 107
7842 Rest. Sal. Loose	2370 Cor-PMV	2349 Cor-PMV	2464 Cor-PMV	1128 SK Set 207
3730 BSK Set 201	2352 Cor-PMV	2347 Cor-PMV	Followed by 12	3725 BSK Set 207
6569 BCK Set 28	2329 Cor-PMV	2358 Cor-PMV	Electric and 10	
1315 SO Set 432	2350 Cor-PMV	2356 Cor-PMV	Steam, Nos.:	
5637 CK Set 270	2472 Cor-PMV	4066 BSK Loose	3732 BSK Set 179	

North of Culham heading for Oxford and eventually Handborough for Blenheim', 30 January 1965. (Note - the station has since been renamed 'Hanborough'.) Photos - Michael Roach

* The title 'Southern Engineman' is currently not available'.

For those of us who were around at the time, we will all have our particular memories of July 1967. For me it was not really believing that steam would actually finish from 10 July. I was then travelling daily by train to school in Southampton and fully expected steam engines if not working, at least to be present at Eastleigh for some weeks afterwards.

However, that Monday morning, 10 July 1967, I was in for a shock. As we sped past the expanse of Eastleigh there was nothing. I would learn later some facts: that the last engines at Eastleigh were actually waiting by the coaling stage so keeping the shed clear, and the reason for this - well simply that the men had been warned, 'The contractors will be in first thing Monday morning to demolish the shed, if you want it and don't take it with you, they will claim it'. Within days, certainly less than a week, the shed had gone, razed to the ground. I do not recall the demolition of the office block, water tower and coaling stage, but now know they too disappeared almost as rapidly: a need to make things easier (I have since discovered) for pilots coming in to land at the airport.

So where is this going, well just to say that nearly fifty years later a snippet of conversation revealed a slim chance that steam might not quite have finished before midnight on Sunday 9 July there is every chance a steam engine was working a revenue earning train on 'Electric Monday', 10 July 1967, albeit for a short distance and for a short time.

Many like me will have read John Bird's excellent account 'Southern Steam Sunset'. In this he describes the last months, weeks, days and even hours of SR steam working. So far as Eastleigh is concerned he recounts that at the very end the following engines remained at the site, Nos 34040, 34044, 34102, 73085 and 76066. A few days later some of these had been removed to the storage sites at Salisbury/Weymouth leaving Nos 34040, 73085 and a newcomer, No 76063. So where does No 76063 fit in? Indeed this is the very clue to what follows.

We have to assume the actual engines numbers are correct because this would certainly fit. Speaking to an about to retire driver from Eastleigh in 2014, he recounted that when he started on the railway in August 1968 he recalled speaking to an ex-fireman, then still a railwayman who recounted he had fired the last steam engine to arrive at Eastleigh - after midnight on the morning of Monday 10 July. Our ex-fireman (now sadly deceased so engine details cannot be confirmed) commented that the driver and himself had worked a parcels train from Waterloo as far as Eastleigh where the engine was uncoupled to run to shed. This was around 1.00 a.m. in the morning. It seems very unlikely this would have been a booked working so the steam engine must have been a last minute substitute for a failed diesel / electric. There is no information as to the engine, but might it be No 76063? Our fireman friend recalled that when they arrived at the depot they were told to leave the engine on the disposal pit, not to replenish the tender and not to bother to clean the fire, 'Just to fill the boiler up and go'. He remembered the incident not just for this which was in itself unusual, but also because walking across the shed it was absolutely deserted, there was not a soul around, no doubt the first time ever it had been in this state since having opened 60-odd years earlier. Why it was so quiet is easily explained: at midnight the signing-on point for drivers and from that time 'second-men' moved from the shed to the station, as this was after midnight that is why it was deserted.

John Bird recounts a not dissimilar incident at Nine Elms where it was rumoured a single steam engine was kept at the ready over the night of 9/10 July just in case the breakdown-train had been required during the night hours - it wasn't.

So was this and our Eastleigh incident proof Southern steam did not quite finish at midnight on 9 July, or is it just an amusing piece of folklore we may wish to hang on to? Personally I know I would like to believe it.